The Power of Your Story
For Men
Participant Manual

THE POWER
of your story
for Men

Participant Manual

Rob Fischer & Perry Underwood

ABANON.org
Abortion Anonymous

The Power of Your Story For Men
Participant's Manual

ISBN-13:978-1542877459

Interior layout by Kim Gardell
Cover design by Kim Gardell

TABLE OF CONTENTS

FOREWORD

Recently, I (Rob) was meeting with a friend in a coffee shop when he shared with me his abortion experience. He had tried to "stuff" his memory of it, but it came back to haunt him now in an unexpected way, 21 years later. He expressed profound sorrow, grief and shame over his abortion.

My friend is not alone. Approximately one in three men in America is post-abortive. Also, our society has been very schizophrenic about abortion. On the one hand, abortion has been legalized, euphemized, and its consequences played down. On the other hand, millions of men and women find themselves—sometimes many years later—deeply ashamed and remorseful over their abortion.

As a result of these mixed messages about abortion, most men and women are silent about their abortion, choosing rather to bear its shame and pain alone. Often, men and women chose to medicate their pain from an abortion in self-destructive ways. What many are discovering, however, is that the only way to remedy the pain and shame of abortion is come clean and share their stories with others.

In doing so, men and women discover that they are not alone. The weight of guilt and shame that they carry is not unique to them, but actually very common. It's just that our culture has discouraged and even made it taboo to share their stories.

For this reason, sharing your abortion story will require great courage on your part. We challenge you to be courageous and tell your story with others in your AbAnon group who will understand and identify with you. This step is crucial for your healing—and theirs.

We're grateful to numerous post-abortive men, without whom we could not have written this curriculum. Some of their stories are recorded here.

Because this curriculum is the joint work of these men, Perry, and me, in many cases we've chosen to identify with you using the plural personal pronoun "we." Please accept our attempt to draw ourselves into your experience in this way.

We invite you to fully enter into this curriculum and the eight sessions you'll spend with other men like yourself. All sessions are gender-specific. We're confident you'll meet some wonderful people and make some good friends in your AbAnon group.

Our hope and desire is that you will experience healing and a new-found hope through this curriculum!

Perry Underwood & Rob Fischer,
January 2017

THE WARM-UP

We know that men do not "have" abortions, it is a physiological impossibility. But every child has a father and for most women who have had an abortion there is a man in the picture who played some role in the abortion process.

A woman's involvement in an abortion is "all-in." They are involved physically, relationally, emotionally, maternally, spiritually, intellectually and psychologically. But for men their involvement in the abortion process may be one of several possible scenarios.

At one end of the spectrum are men who fathered a child that the mother aborted without his knowledge. In fact, he may not have even known she was pregnant. There are many men walking around today that have fathered an aborted child and they are completely ignorant of the fact.

At the other end of the spectrum are men who forced or coerced their wife, girlfriend or daughter, against her will, into aborting her child. There was no "choice" in the matter. Between these two ends of the spectrum there are a variety of other scenarios. Each situation is a bit different and every man's story is a bit different. How abortion has affected each man is different and how each man processes his role in an abortion will also be different.

This curriculum attempts to deal with as many scenarios of men's roles in abortions as is reasonably possible. The stories shared within this book are specific to the story-tellers' situations, but much of this book is more general. Each man participating in this AbAnon curriculum should glean what he can from material that directly applies to his personal abortion. But for those scenarios covered within this material that are dissimilar to his, each man should look for *principles* to glean and apply those principles wherever possible.

As a warm-up to the eight-session curriculum we are about to share, we ask each AbAnon men's group participant to read (or re-read) Chapter 19 of **The Big Game…**Things Men Should Talk About But Rarely Do. The text below has been taken directly from **The Big Game** by Perry Underwood.

CHAPTER 19—THE ELEPHANT IN THE ROOM

I thought I was done writing this book. I met with my friend and editor, Rob Fischer, and proudly proclaimed, "It is finished." Knowing my sense of accomplishment that accompanied the thrill of completing an enormous task, he graciously convinced me that the book needed one more chapter. Like having a penalty on the final play of a very close football game, my elation was postponed.

Rob said that there was one particular men's issue that had been subtly addressed throughout this book but he felt that the issue needed to be dealt with more directly. He said, "It's like an elephant in the room that affects millions of men yet no one wants to talk about it." He advised me not to dance around the issue but to deal with it head-on.

So before I deal with this issue, please allow me the indulgence of one more story.

Throughout this book I've touched on the various phases of my working history but here I'd like to offer a recap so you have the proper context of where I'm headed. When I was in eighth grade I began working in the family construction business and continued to do so on weekends, holidays and summer vacations until I graduated from college. After college my wife and I took a job managing seventy-two apartment units and did this for just over one year. After managing the apartments, I accepted a position as Office Manager for a group of physicians. I held this position for about three years.

Next, I started a financial consulting business which evolved into a real estate business. This was my profession for almost thirty years. About five years before getting out of the real estate business I launch an internet marketing business. I eventually sold the real estate business so that I could devote full time to the internet marketing business which has since shut down. I still believe that the internet marketing concept we launched is far and away better than any internet marketing business operating today. But the million dollars invested in the business by me and a few friends was far too little to carry the company to the tipping point. Other than the money we lost and the hit to my pride, there was no serious damage as a result.

After shutting down the internet marketing business I began doing business consulting work. Basically companies would hire me to look at whatever seemed to be troubling them and I would develop strategies to cure their ailment. Most problems can be reduced to one of three things: a policy, a practice, or a person. Sometimes solving my client's problem would involve knocking off a competitor or breaking the legs of their employees' union representative. Just kidding.

One of my business consulting clients was a Pregnancy Resource Center. The leadership of this organization seemed convinced that most, if not all women and men involved in an abortion were adversely affected by it. Yet in their city where abortions numbered 2000 annually, only fifteen to twenty women each year attended any sort of post-abortion recovery/healing group. Typically, the number of men participating in these groups each year was zero.

After reviewing their problem I came to the conclusion that there were three *possible reasons* why so few people were participating in post-abortion healing programs. Either:

1) My client was incorrect in their assumption that most people involved in abortions are adversely affected, or…

2) Post-abortive individuals were unaware of their need for my client's services, or…

3) Post-abortive individuals saw their need for my client's services but were unaware that my client offered these services.

If item #1 were true it would simply be a matter doing some research and providing some answers. If items #2 or #3 were true it would be a matter of developing a more effective marketing strategy.

I surmised that another possible reason for low participation could be ineffective curriculum but ruled that possibility out due to lack of participants to begin with. However, it was clear that none of the few post-abortive group participants were returning to subsequent groups, bringing with them a post-abortive friend or family member. This was an indication that the curriculum may indeed be an issue. In other words, as with any business, there is usually some sort of problem if existing clients are not referring other clients to that business.

For eight months I read everything I could get my hands on related to the topic of abortion. I conducted several focus groups of post-abortive women. I heard or read dozens if not hundreds of stories of men and women involved in an abortion. And I came to the following conclusions:

1) **No person, man or woman, has been involved in an abortion experience without being adversely affected.** Of the hundreds of abortion stories I have heard I have yet to hear a single one where the abortion participant *did not* develop some sort of behavioral issue *after* the experience. My client's assumption was correct.

2) I do not claim or pretend to be any sort of behavioral expert, but I have done enough research and have interviewed enough people to know that what I'm about to say is undoubtedly true. Some of the more common post-abortive behavioral issues I've seen include: abuse of alcohol; addictions to sex, pornography, legal and illegal drugs or gambling; sleep disorders; excessive or unhealthy drive to excel at work, school or sports, excessive pro-life or pro-choice activism; anger issues; a change from a heterosexual to a gay or lesbian lifestyle; and an aversion to being around children or pregnant women.

   But the interesting thing about the people I have spoken with is that *they rarely recognize the connection between their abortion and their behavioral deviations.* And many do not see their behavioral deviations as a problem at all; they simply chalk it up as who they are. **In short, people do not readily see their need for post-abortion healing because they see their**

behavioral issue as the problem rather than their behavioral issue being a symptom of the underlying abortion. My client had a marketing problem.

3) It is very rare when someone who abuses alcohol wakes up one morning and says to himself, "Self, you have an alcohol addiction. You need to enroll in Alcoholics Anonymous." Before attending any program to get away from the alcohol he must first reach a breaking point. He must first encounter the potential loss of something he values more than the alcohol. Among other things, this could be his marriage, his job, his ability to drive, or his reputation.

The same is true of any other addiction or behavioral issue. To effectuate change of behavior people must be "pushed" or "compelled" to make the change. Abortion recovery is no different. Organizations can advertise, promote and market post-abortion recovery programs until they are blue in the face but the results will remain dismal. **It does no good to invite people to a post-abortive recovery group; people must be brought to a group by someone who loves them enough to make it happen.** This too is an issue that must be resolved through a more effective marketing strategy.

Another discovery I made in my abortion research is that the people who indeed were able to move past their abortion experience all had three things in common. First, they attended any one of a number of post-abortion recovery programs. Second, there was always an element of forgiveness from God and the ability to forgive themselves. Third, there was some sort of deliberate acknowledgement of the humanity of the aborted child and an intentional grieving process.

All this I learned while doing research for my client, the Pregnancy Resource Center. But now I was in a quandary. I learned that poor participation in post-abortion recovery groups was not only the experience of my client but that poor attendance in post-abortion recovery groups was almost universal. This problem was common in every major US city as well as cities all over the world.

Then I heard that very quiet yet forceful voice in my head saying, "Now that you know what you know, what are you going to do about it?"

The argument was on. I felt that God wanted me to create an organization for the post-abortive modeled after the granddaddy of all anonymous organizations, Alcoholics Anonymous. I *did not* want to do this. God and I argued. I lost the argument. So in 2013 I founded an organization, Abortion Anonymous, Inc. (AbAnon). More about AbAnon can be found at ***http://www.abanon.org***.

When starting AbAnon, my original intention was to simply serve on the Board of Directors for a period of time to help get it started then I would get out of the way. I thought then, and still do today that the Executive Director of AbAnon needs to be an articulate, attractive, educated, post-abortive, woman. I strike out on all five characteristics. But God and our Board of Directors, in their infinite wisdom, have placed me in this position for a season.

Now, back to my friend Rob Fischer and the elephant in the room.

I'm sure you have figured out by now but the elephant in the room that no one seems to want to talk about is the devastation caused by abortion and the role we men have played in allowing it to happen.

When it comes to abortion, I believe that many men have acted selfishly or cowardly. Selfishly, because we've put our dreams, pride and desires above our God-given responsibility to provide and protect.

Cowardly, because we won't speak the truth about abortion because we fear what others will think or say about us.

Some of you reading this book are of the opinion that abortion is a good thing and are clueless as to how wrong and evil it is. You might consider yourself to be pro-choice and proud of it. I even know of pro-choice ministers and priests. If this describes you, then I would challenge you to open your heart and mind by reading a few books that offer an opinion contrary to yours. One such book is a book which I've written titled **Change the Shame;** *Continuing the Battle for Civil Rights.*

Some of you reading this book are probably of the opinion that most abortions are wrong but you are okay with abortion if the mother was raped or the child has a disability. If you fit this category, I offer the same challenge I gave the men described in the paragraph above. As humans we tend to believe whatever we choose to believe regardless of how overwhelming the evidence is to the contrary. But if our hearts and minds are open God can change them.

Undoubtedly, some of you reading this book are pro-life but, like I used to be, you are closet pro-lifers. I was pro-life but I wasn't about to say anything to anyone that might create an awkward situation or put me in a bad light. Quite honestly, I was a coward about what other people thought; especially when it came to people I did business with.

Some of you reading this book are pro-life and vocal about being so. But I can only applaud your pro-life position if it is accompanied by compassion, love and forgiveness towards those who have been involved in an abortion. We have all done things we are not proud of. Something about casting stones comes to mind. Spouting *God's grace* without understanding *one's guilt* is just as worthless as critically pointing out *one's guilt* without offering *His grace*. Both scenarios are equally ineffective.

Some of you reading this book may have fathered a child and your child was aborted without you knowing about it until it was too late. I can only imagine the pain, anger or helplessness you must have felt. My hope is that you can process those emotions properly and come to the point where you are able to forgive your child's mother.

Some of you reading this book were quiet bystanders while your wife, girlfriend or daughter had an abortion and you said nothing or did very little to defend the child. You bought into the lie that abortion is a woman's health issue and since you don't have a uterus you must keep your mouth shut and your opinions to yourself. But just as women have maternal instincts to nurture and care, men have paternal instincts to provide and protect. I've learned from so many testimonials that to stand by and do nothing while your child or grandchild is taken can haunt you for your entire life.

Some of you reading this book were active participants in an abortion. You may have begged, coerced, manipulated or even forced your wife, girlfriend or daughter into having an abortion. You may have paid for the abortion, driven the car to the clinic or were present during the procedure. Perhaps the details surrounding the event that happened many years ago are burned into your memory as if they had taken place yesterday. You may still be trying to convince yourself that it was the right thing to do and justify your actions. But deep within your soul you know that what you did was wrong.

Man or woman, those who have played a role in an abortion will never be all that God intends them to be until they have properly processed the abortion and found forgiveness, healing and freedom. The enemy wants you to quietly remain in your shame and guilt. You see, the enemy knows that once you are set free, your story has the power to free dozens or possibly hundreds of other men.

If you have been a bystander or have actively played a role in an abortion, I want to encourage you participate in a post-abortion recovery program for men. I know, you're probably thinking, "I'm tough and I've dealt with it in my own way." You may know that you have been forgiven by God, and you may have even forgiven yourself. But my guess is that unless you've been part of a post-abortion recovery group, you have not properly dealt with your abortion. If this is the case, there are probably some behavioral issues that you struggle with on a regular basis. If that's true of you, attend a group to help yourself. If I am mistaken, great, attend such a group to help others.

You are here today as part of this AbAnon Men's Group. You might be here as a result of reading *The Big Game*, by the encouragement of a friend or for some other reason. We don't know what brought you here but the main thing is that you *are* here. It is our sincere hope that you take these next few weeks seriously and let the healing begin.

SESSION ONE

WELCOME

_____ and _____ will be your facilitators for the next eight weeks. You are very courageous for taking this step toward processing your role in an abortion. We're glad you're here.

INTRODUCTIONS

- Name
- Whatever you'd like to share with us to help us get to know you.
- What would you like to take away from your experience over the next eight weeks?

OVER THE NEXT EIGHT WEEKS, WE WILL TALK ABOUT

- Your abortion story and the role you played
- How your role in an abortion may have affected you
- Ways you may have coped with your abortion involvement
- Your relationships
- Your child (or grandchild)
- Common emotions surrounding abortion involvement
- God & faith
- Healing & forgiveness

ESTABLISH GROUP NORMS

We like to establish group norms or ground rules by which we agree to conduct our meetings together. This way we all have the same expectations and can get the most from this experience. Some group norms we see as essential are:

Keep confidences — What we say here stays here. We pledge to keep confidences and ask the same of each member of the group.

Be present and ready — Attend all the sessions (except in an emergency). Your presence here is not only important for you, but for the other participants as well. Being present includes keeping up with the light reading or homework between sessions.

Be respectful — We agree to respect each other: our individual situations, our ethnicity, our faiths, the choices we've made, the things we may say, how we each process our abortion involvement.

Function as a team — We agree to function as a team: no one dominates the conversation; we listen to each other; we're here to assist, encourage and care for each other.

Be humble — We're not here to judge or *fix* each other. Sometimes the way we suppress our own need is by comparing ourselves to someone else or trying to fix them.

What else would you like to set down as a group norm?

DISCLAIMER

We recognize that every person is different and working through issues surrounding your role in an abortion usually occurs over time. Our sincere hope is that you will experience some measure of healing through this 8-session experience.

Also, we openly declare that our facilitators and co-facilitators are not professional counselors or life coaches. But having personally experienced a man's role in an abortion, they are passionate about providing a safe, supportive environment for others.

Any profits from the sale of the Participant Manuals go to cover the cost of printing, shipping and the support and expansion of AbAnon.

Abortion Anonymous, Inc. (AbAnon) is a registered, 501c3 not-for-profit organization and is financed primarily through the generous donations of financial partners.

If you are actively harming yourself or having suicidal thoughts, please seek the help of a professional counselor immediately. We can discretely help you locate a counselor if you like. This workshop is not intended to replace professional counseling or therapy.

INTRODUCTION — THE POWER OF YOUR STORY: FOR MEN

Welcome! We are so glad you've chosen to join us for this eight-week experience designed to help you process your role in an abortion experience. Be assured that we will maintain the utmost confidentiality as you participate with this small group of men.

All of the facilitators or group leaders come with their own story regarding their role in an abortion and are in various stages of working through their involvement. Your facilitators are all volunteers and do not receive payment for leading a group.

The manual recognizes that although there are some basic issues that we all experience, or need to face, each man processes his role in an abortion in a different way. Some express the need for healing and others do not.

Whatever it is you seek with regard to your role in an abortion, some sort of change is inevitable. Change can be difficult and scary, but necessary if we want to experience different outcomes than we're currently experiencing. Please avail yourself of every method and opportunity that we provide to help facilitate your desired change.

AbAnon is not an overtly religious organization and does not represent a particular religion, denomination or faith. Anyone, regardless of their faith or lack thereof, who has had an abortion or played a role in an abortion, is welcome to our gender-specific programs.

However, part of our 8-week program involves discussion about God, faith and forgiveness. Thousands of people have found change and healing through faith and we would be remiss in our responsibility if we failed to include God and faith in our curriculum.

Some of what we'll be discussing together will be inherently difficult to discuss, but remember, we're all in this together.

Finally, we understand that many men just do not like to read. For those of you who do not have a passion for reading take heart, this first session has the most reading by far. In this first session we are attempting to lay a solid foundation and a clear understanding for the importance of your being here. The reading in this first session will take about twice as long as the future sessions.

HOW THE PARTICIPANT MANUAL WORKS

Each weekly session or chapter has pre-work that you will complete *prior to* the next session. For instance, if you turn to Session Two in this Manual, you'll see that it begins with Mike's Story, followed by some discussion questions and then a short reading on why it's so vital to share your story.

Some of the chapters also contain projects. Please do this homework early in the week so that you're not scrambling at the last minute to finish. Take your time and seek to gain all you can from this experience. The more you invest, the more you'll take away.

MEN AND ABORTION

The following article was written by David C. Reardon, Ph.D. and titled *Forgotten Fathers and Their Unforgettable Children*. This article was published in June of 2015 as part of a **Special Report on Men and Abortion** by *The Elliott Institute News*.

> *In the early 1970s, Arthur Shostak accompanied his partner to a well-groomed suburban abortion clinic. They had both agreed abortion was best. But sitting in the waiting room proved to be a "bruising experience." By the time he left the clinic, he was shocked by about how deeply disturbed he had become.*

A professor of sociology at Drexel University in Philadelphia, Shostak spent the subsequent ten years studying the abortion experience of men. His study included a survey of 1,000 men who accompanied their wives or girlfriends to abortion clinics.

Shostak's study was published in Men and Abortion: Lessons, Losses and Love, in 1984. The value of this study is limited to reporting mostly the short term reactions of men to the pregnancy and the decision to abort. In addition, because of the selection process, this study did not reflect the attitudes or experiences of men who did not accompany their partners to the abortion clinic–which could be because they were unaware of the pregnancy and abortion, because they were casual or unsupportive partners, or because they were opposed to the abortion. Despite these significant limitations, Shostak's study, using the largest group of men ever surveyed about their abortions, is still the benchmark study in this understudied field.

Shostak reported that the majority of the men surveyed in clinic waiting rooms felt isolated, angry at their partners or themselves, and were concerned about the physical and emotional damage abortion might cause their partner. Only about one-fourth of the men stated that they had offered to pay the costs of raising the child if the woman didn't abort. Half of the single men said they offered to marry (if) their female partner continued the pregnancy.

Shostak's study found that abortion is far more stressful for men than the public would generally suppose. More than one in four equated abortion to murder. Slightly over 80 percent said they had already begun to think about the child that might have been born (with 29 percent saying they had been fantasizing about the child "frequently"), 68 percent believed men involved in abortions "did not have an easy time of it," and 47 percent worried about having disturbing thoughts afterwards. Shostak reported that many men began to cry during the interview.

The overwhelming majority, 83 percent, opposed any legal restrictions on abortion, and 45 percent stated that they had urged an abortion (48 percent of unmarried men and 37 percent of the married men). When asked if the man and woman should have an equal say in the decision, 80 percent of married men agreed compared to 58 percent of single men. Many expressed frustration and anger about the failure of women to consider their wishes and feelings. They felt isolated from the decision and–especially if they opposed the abortion–emasculated and powerless.

In a subsequent interview Shostak said:

Most of the men I talk to think about the abortion years after it is over. They feel sad, they feel curious, they feel a lot of things; but usually they have talked to no one about it. It's a taboo.... With a man, if he wants to shed a tear, he had better do it privately. If he feels that the abortion had denied him his child, he had better work through it himself. He does not share his pain with a clergyman, a minister; he does not share it with a close male friend.... It just stays with him. And it stays for a long time.[1]

Research Shows A Range of Negative Reactions

Other studies contribute to this grim picture. In a random telephone survey conducted in 1989 by the Los Angeles Times, only 7 percent of males and 8 percent of females admitted having a prior history of abortion. (This is well under one-third of the expected rate, indicating that most people feel a need to conceal

---

1   Thomas Strahan, "Portraits of Post-Abortive Fathers Devastated by the Abortion Experience," *Assoc. for Interdisciplinary Research in Values and Social Change*, 7(3), Nov/Dec 1994.

their involvement in a past abortion, even in an anonymous survey.) Of those admitting to an abortion, men were significantly more likely to admit to negative feelings. Two of every three men reported feelings of guilt compared to 56 percent of the women. Over one-third of the men who admitted involvement in a past abortion said they regretted the abortion compared to one-quarter of the women.[2]

An interview-based study of inmates at a medium security prison found that male prisoners with a history of involvement in abortion had a generally negative view of abortion. Most reported that it had been, and continued to be, a negative psychological experience for themselves and their partners.[3]

Men have reported a large number of problems that they claim were a direct result of their abortion experience. These include broken relationships, sexual dysfunction, substance abuse, self-hate, risk taking and suicidal behavior, increasing feelings of grief over time, feelings of helplessness, guilt, depression, greater tendencies toward becoming angry and violent, and feelings connected to a sense of lost manhood.[4]

According to Dr. Vincent Rue, one of the nation's most experienced psychologists in the field of post-abortion issues:

Induced abortion reinforces defective problem solving on the part of the male by encouraging detachment, desertion, and irresponsibility.... Abortion rewrites the rules of masculinity. While a male is expected to be strong, abortion makes him feel weak. A male is expected to be responsible, yet abortion

2   George Skelton, "Many in Survey Who Had Abortion Cite Guilt Feelings," *Los Angeles Times*, March 19, 1989, p28.
3   Lindy A. Pierce, "Abortion Attitudes and Experiences in a Group of Male Prisoners," *Assoc. for Interdisciplinary Research*, 6(2), Jan/Feb 1994.
4   Strahan, "Portraits," op. cit.

encourages him to act without concern for the innocent and to destroy any identifiable and undesirable outcomes of his sexual decision making and/or attachments.... Whether or not the male was involved in the abortion decision, his inability to function in a socially prescribed manner (i.e., to protect and provide) leaves him wounded and confused.

Typical male grief responses include remaining silent and grieving alone. In the silence, a male can harbor guilt and doubts about his ability to protect himself and those he loves.... Some become depressed and/or anxious, others compulsive, controlling, demanding and directing. Still others become enraged, and failure in any relationship can trigger repressed hostility from their disenfranchised grief.... [The act of running from the grief process] fosters denial and forces a male to become a "fugitive" from life, loving, and healing. A guilt-ridden, tormented male does not easily love or accept love.[5]

Abortion Impacts Men's Relationships

Because abortion affects both women and men, it must necessarily have an Impact on couple and family relationships. Most research supports the conclusion that the vast majority of unmarried couples who participate in an abortion end their relationships within a year, often within weeks. While the outcome for married couples is more mixed, many report that their abortion led them to divorce. One study has found that unsatisfactory or mediocre marital adjustments before an abortion are predictive of greater marital or sexual maladjustments after an abortion.[6]

---

5   Vincent Rue, "The Effects of Abortion on Men," *Ethics & Medics* 21(4):3-4, 1996.

6   E. M. Belsey, et al., "Predictive factors in emotional response to Abortion: Kings Termination Study, IV," *Social Science and Medicine* 11:71-82 (1977).

Abortion has never been known to solve any relationship problems. The only time couples report feeling closer after an abortion is when they have mutually shared feelings of grief and regret about having aborted their child. In short, the relief of being freed from an unplanned pregnancy never binds a couple closer together, but honestly shared remorse can.

While broken relationships after an abortion are often interpreted as the result of women rejecting the uncommitted male, other dynamics also contribute to this problem. In most cases, the abortion is relegated to "something we don't talk about." This non-communication zone stifles the relationship and establishes a pattern for hiding other feelings as well.

Males may feel especially bound by a code of silence. They are likely to believe it is their manly duty not to aggravate their lover's emotional recovery with any expression of their own doubts or grief. In general, there is a need, as individuals and as a couple, to hold to the party line: "We did the right thing."

At the same time, the man and the woman are each likely to be experiencing different levels of regret, guilt, resentment, and recrimination. If one is coping relatively well, this may not sit well with the partner who is saddened or depressed. Conversely, signs of depression may aggravate the guilt and resentment of the non-depressed party who feels unfairly blamed for the abortion.

The less affected person may also become confused and frustrated if his or her partner begins to experience sexual dysfunction, substance abuse, uncharacteristic workaholic tendencies, disengagement from previously enjoyed activities, or other post-abortion reactions.

Such dynamics may underlie more frequent and bitter fighting, over unrelated issues, which may even culminate in physical violence.[7] In one of the first studies to examine the impact of abortion on men's relationships, men who were involved in an abortion with a current partner were more likely to report domestic violence; to feel that their lives would be better if the relationship ended; to have difficulty with jealousy or drug use; and to report arguing about children, jealousy and drugs.[8]

If a past abortion is kept secret in subsequent relationships, this secret may have a destructive effect on the new couple's relationship and their family unit. Secrets signify a lack of trust, which acted upon, becomes distrust. Unable to share a secret pain, the secret keeper is unable to experience the full acceptance and love of family members who are being kept "in the dark." The secret thus exerts a constant hold over the couple and the family; it is an obstacle to more complete intimacy.

The work of some family therapists suggests that abortion may also create an unsettling ambiguity about one's "family boundary." After an abortion, members of the family who are aware of the abortion may develop a cognitive or emotional difficulty knowing who is in and who is out of the family system.(8) For example, every time post-abortive men and women are asked how many children they have, they may flinch. Should the aborted child be acknowledged and numbered among their offspring? Similarly, siblings of an aborted child may experience similar unsettling feelings about the proper dimensions of their family.

---

7   See "Abortion and Domestic Violence," *The Post-Abortion Review* 4(2-3):13-15,1996.
8   P.K. Coleman, V.M. Rue, C.T. Coyle, "Induced abortion and intimate relationship quality in the Chicago Health and Social Life Survey," *Public Health* (2009)doi:10, 1016/ j. puhe. 2009 .01.005.

Usually, when a family member dies the rest of the family en-
gages in public and familial grief process, which if successful,
"closes the wound." But proper closure following the loss of a
miscarried or aborted child is much more difficult because our
culture resists, and is even hostile to, acknowledging the reality
that abortion involves the loss of a child–a member of a family.

We are here to acknowledge and empathize with you as you process your role in an abortion experience. You are not alone.

In fact, according to the Guttmacher Institute, 21 percent of all preg- nancies end in abortion in the US.[9] And between 35-40 percent of all women alive in the US today have had at least one abortion.[10] It is safe to assume that the number of men involved in an abortion would be similar. Each year, over 1 million abortions occur in the US. As of the writing of this curriculum in 2016, about 60 million abortions have been performed since its legalization in 1973.[11]

POST ABORTIVE STRESS SYNDROME

AbAnon is in the process of gathering data from men involved in abor- tion but since men's role in abortion is a vastly understudied topic, we will share with you some conclusions as to how abortion affects women taken directly from **The Power of Your Story**, the AbAnon cur- riculum for women. It reads as follows:

Joan Appleton was the head nurse at Commonwealth [Abortion] Clinic. Joan was a very active member in the National Organization

9   Guttmacher Institute, "Induced Abortion in the United States," July 2014, http://www. guttmacher.org/pubs/fb_induced_abortion.html.
10   Guttmacher Institute.
11   Guttmacher Institute.

for Women (NOW). As a registered nurse, she felt she had a wonderful opportunity to practice and voice her beliefs in pro-choice.[12]

She was convinced that pro-choice was truly the best thing for women and began to work more and more with organizations like Planned Parenthood, NARAL and NAF. As a nurse she was issuing birth control pills to women after abortions and comments, "This is where I learned the real business, the real work of the abortion industry."[13]

Joan explains that abortion clinic workers handed out low-dose birth control pills with a high failure rate. They also neglected to tell women that taking a birth control pill while on antibiotics interferes with the action of the pill, making it useless. In this way, when their birth control failed, they were able to get more women to come in for abortions.[14]

Joan explains, "I often saw women who were injured emotionally by abortion. However, my supervisor told me, 'If she's having a problem after her abortion, it's because she was having a problem before her abortion.'"[15]

But it kept bothering Joan while she was head nurse at the clinic. "Why was it such an emotional trauma for a woman and such a difficult decision, if it was a natural thing to do? If it was right, why was it so difficult? I had to ask myself that all the time. I counseled these women so well, they were so sure of their decision. So why were they coming back now, months and years later, psychological wrecks?"[16]

Joan continues to explain that in the pro-choice movement and abortion industry, "We deny that there is any post-abortion syndrome. Yet

12   Clinic Quotes, "Former Clinic Worker Joan Appleton," September 11, 2012, http://clinic-quotes.com/former-clinic-worker-joan-appleton/
13   Clinic Quotes.
14   Clinic Quotes.
15   Clinic Quotes.
16   Clinic Quotes.

it is real, and they do come back, and I couldn't deny their presence, and their numbers were increasing, and I kept asking, Why?"[17]

Joan soon realized that she wasn't helping women at all. Joan writes:

"If I was right, why are they suffering? What have we done? We created a monster, and now we don't know what to do with it. We created a monster so that we could now be pawns to the abortion industry, those of us women who really, really still believe in women's rights. Those of us who still believe in care and are pro-woman, who still believe that we are worth something, we are intelligent, we aren't doormats, we aren't something to be used, and we used ourselves. We abused ourselves."[18]

We refer to these very real psychological effects as Post Abortion Stress Syndrome (or PASS). Proponents of abortion often deny the existence of PASS. This brings additional pressure to bear on women who are feeling the negative effects of abortion, but are told that their feelings are not real or necessary.[19,20]

However, Susanne Babbel, PhD, MFT, a psychologist specializing in trauma and depression has the following to say: "No matter your philosophical, religious, or political views on abortion, the fact of the matter is, the actual experience can affect women not only on a personal level but can potentially have psychological repercussions."[21]

---

17   Clinic Quotes.

18   Clinic Quotes.

19   National Abortion Federation, "Post-Abortion Syndrome," 2010, https://www.prochoice.org/about_abortion/myths/post_abortion_syndrome.html.

20   Christina Martin, "Tears Streamed Down Her Face as She Talked about Her Abortion, but Abortion Doesn't Hurt Women?" LifeNews.com, July 30, 2014, http://www.lifenews.com/2014/07/30/tears-streamed-down-herface- as-she-talked-about-her-abortion-but-abortion-doesnt-hurt-women/.

21   Susanne Babbel, PhD, MFT, "Post Abortion Stress Syndrome (PASS) – Does it Exist?" Psychology Today, October 25, 2010, http://www.psychologytoday.com/blog/somatic-psychology/201010/post-abortion-stress-syndrome-pass-does-it-exist..

Dr. Babbel goes on to explain:

Post Abortion Stress Syndrome (PASS) is the name that has been given to the psychological aftereffects of abortion, based on Post Traumatic Stress Disorder (PTSD). It is important to note that this is not a term that has been accepted by the American Psychiatric Association or the American Psychological Association. Nevertheless, any event that causes trauma can indeed result in PTSD, and abortion is no exception.[22]

PASS

How widespread is Post Abortion Stress Syndrome (PASS) and the trauma on women (and men) brought on by abortion?

Nearly everyone agrees that feelings of loss and depression follow at some point after an abortion. Post Abortion Stress Syndrome (PASS) describes more severe and extensive trauma that may include: [23]

- ☐ Self-harm, strong suicidal thoughts or suicide attempts

- ☐ Increase in dangerous and/or unhealthy activities (alcohol/drug abuse, anorexia/bulimia, compulsive over-eating, cutting, casual and indifferent sex and other inappropriate risk-taking behaviors)

- ☐ Depression that is stronger than just 'a little sadness or the blues'

- ☐ Inability to perform normal self-care activities

---

22   Susanne Babbel.
23   AfterAbortion.com, "What is PASS?" http://afterabortion.com/pass_details. html.

☐ Inability to function normally in her job or in school.

☐ Inability to take care of or relate to her existing children or function normally in her other relationships (i.e. with a spouse, partner, other family members or friends)

☐ A desire to immediately get pregnant and 'replace' the baby that was aborted.

In addition to the above, PASS sometimes does not appear until months or even many years after an abortion and may continue for months and even years. Other short- and long-term PASS symptoms may include:[24]

☐ Emotions, and dealing with emotional issues

☐ Anxiety and panic disorder

☐ Difficulty sleeping and sleeping problems

☐ Disturbing dreams and/or nightmares

☐ Problems with phobias, or increase in severity of existing phobias

☐ Repeated unplanned pregnancies with additional abortions

☐ Repeated unplanned pregnancies carried to term

☐ "Atonement marriage," where the woman marries the partner from the abortion, to help justify the abortion

---

24   AfterAbortion.com.

☐ Distress at the sight of or socializing with other pregnant women, other people's babies and children

☐ Codependence and inability to make decisions easily

☐ Problems with severe and disproportionate anger

☐ Distress and problems with later pregnancy

☐ Added emotional issues and problems when dealing with future infertility or other physical complications resulting from the abortion

☐ Unhealthy obsession with excelling at work or school to justify the abortion

☐ Obsessive Pro-life or Pro-choice activism

☐ A lesbian lifestyle

PASS SELF-ASSESSMENT

Obviously, not all of the PASS symptoms for women apply to men, so keep that in mind when you do your homework for next session. You will be asked to come back to these two lists of PASS symptoms in order to assess your own situation.

WHERE DO WE GO FROM HERE?

Some of you may be thinking, "I've been trying to put my abortion role behind me for years. Why would I want to revisit that experience again? I just want to put it behind me and forget about it." Others may be processing their abortion role in a different way that's difficult to describe at this time. That's okay.

In the following seven weeks of *The Power of Your Story: For Men,* we want to join with you in processing your role in an abortion. We'll provide you with tools and strategies for doing so. We want to help you find answers, support you, and offer you hope.

HOMEWORK FOR THE NEXT SESSION

Your homework for next week will go rather quickly. Please review the PASS symptoms listed above and check all the symptoms that apply to your situation. Feel free to list any other symptoms that apply to you that are not listed. Next, please read Session TWO and complete the tasks outlined at the end of Session Two before our next meeting. You will find these on pages 37-47 in this manual. You may wish to turn there and go over these now.

LOGISTICS

We'll meet here each week for seven more weeks at _____(time).

SESSION TWO

MIKE'S STORY

Please read the following true story and reflect on the questions that follow.

My story is one that is probably not all that unusual. It was 1976 or 1977. I came from a military family; my Dad was career Navy and my Mom was Japanese.

I was dating a girl in high school who was from a large Catholic family which included thirteen siblings. Although her family was Catholic they weren't what I would call "devout."

After dating a while, my girlfriend and I became sexually active but we were young and thought that all we needed to do for birth control was the Catholic rhythm method. This method seemed to work for everyone else. Well, as you can imagine, after a few months my girlfriend was now pregnant.

We were very embarrassed to tell our parents...tons of shame. But both sets of parents handled the news with surprising calmness and maturity. They simply wanted to know, "Now what?"

As we processed our situation we approached things very matter-of-factly and business-like. I was seventeen years old and was pursuing an Army career. We both felt it was important to finish high school and we were both too young and immature to be parents. Our decision was easy, have an abortion, get rid of the "mass of tissue" before it became a real person. Having the baby was never an option.

We told our parents that we were going to have an abortion. Both sets of parents expressed some disappointment, maybe even some minor objection, but it was our decision and neither set of parents objected very strongly. There was no one ardently defending the child's right to live.

A couple of years later my girlfriend and I got married and are still married after thirty-five years. I spent ten years in the Army and we have three children. I don't think about my abortion very often. I would not say that it has haunted me, or affected our relationship. Like any macho man, I put the abortion behind me and moved on. But at the same time I can't help but wonder if the abortion played a role in a miscarriage that my wife had later on. I also wonder if the abortion had anything to do with my infidelity or my years of addiction to drugs and alcohol. Apparently, these are common reactions to having had an abortion.

I became a church-goer and carried on this pretense for many years. I was a Sunday morning Christian with no real relationship with God. But a few years ago, with the encouragement of a friend, I had a spiritual encounter. I asked God to forgive me of my sins and invited Jesus into my heart. I can't explain what happened, but the next morning when I got up I could tell I was different. A huge weight had been lifted from my shoulders and I was now free from all the guilt and shame I had carried for years. And for some reason I now find it very therapeutic to talk about the abortion.

The abortion is not something that my wife and I had talked about very often, but we were forced to talk about it when our son's girlfriend became pregnant a few years ago. We ardently defended that child's right to live and thankfully it resulted in an open adoption.

The advice I would offer men who have been involved in an abortion is this: like me you probably don't realize it, but don't think for a minute that your abortion is not affecting you and your behavior. Talk about your abortion and the role you played, you'll find it to be quite therapeutic.

—Mike 2015

DISCUSS MIKE'S STORY

1. In what ways can you identify with Mike's story? What were you feeling?

2. In what ways did Mike's role in an abortion affect him?

3. What are you taking away from Mike's story to help you process your abortion experience?

WHY IT'S SO VITAL TO SHARE YOUR STORY

The real freedom we seek is often found in the vulnerability of the secrets we least desire to talk about. – Lee Hudson[25]

When guys get together they talk about many things. Men will talk about things like sports, hunting, their jobs, their wife and kids. If their relationship with these men is strong enough they might even dare to venture into the topics of religion or politics. But even daring to discuss religion or politics usually requires some understanding as to where the other guy stands.

Even more taboo than politics or religion is the subject of abortion. Men just don't talk about it. Yet, as we read earlier, one in three men have played a role in an abortion and for many men abortion is a traumatic experience of loss. Whether this loss is conscious or shoved away in the back of their man-vault, it is very real. Just as women, men will experience guilt, anger and shame from their involvement in an abortion.

---

25   Lee Hudson, *Plains Thunder: the Invitation from Jesus to Real Worship* (Anchorage, AK: Saint Elias Music, LLC, 2011), p. 35.

Depending on the role played by the father of the aborted child, the extent of these emotions will vary. The man who forced his girlfriend to get an abortion may feel more shame than anger. The man who learned about the abortion of his child after the fact may feel more anger than shame. We will deal in great detail with each of these emotions in later sessions, but this session deals with men who felt powerless or voiceless in the decision to abort.

You may have never talked about your role in an abortion with other men. Even if you have, you probably have never talked about the loss you felt or the emotions that linger. But everyone in this AbAnon Group has a similar experience. Talking about your experience is a crucial first step in processing your role in an abortion.

HOW WE LOST OUR VOICE

Men are born with the instinct to provide and protect and men who fail to do so are viewed with contempt. Yet when it comes to men's role in abortion, this instinct to provide and protect is nullified by today's culture. The same culture that demands that fathers provide and protect has stripped men of this responsibility when it comes to abortion. Many men who have fathered an aborted child have expressed that they felt "voiceless." To be voiceless is to be powerless and vulnerable.

There are at least three ways that your abortion experience may have left you without a voice. First, many men demanded or were responsible for pushing the abortion and many of these men feel deeply ashamed for doing so. Shame causes us to hide what we've done. We live in fear of being found out or exposed. This fear prevents us from speaking the truth about our past and even may prompt us to lie about it. In this way, we feel *gagged* in terms of talking about our role in an abortion.

Second, many men feel that their opinion didn't matter, that they had no power in determining the future of the baby they fathered. Their child was taken without their input, consent, or possibly even their knowledge. Their child was taken and there wasn't anything he could do or say to prevent it. In cases where the father could have prevented the abortion many men felt pressured to go along with it by the mother, her parents, his parents, a sibling, well-meaning friends, a doctor, or social worker. In these cases, someone else spoke on behalf of the man and made the decision for him.

Finally, the voice of our culture speaks out in favor of abortion so loudly and pervasively that it overwhelms or drowns out our voice. For instance, the voice of the media and many people assert:

- "Abortion is a good choice."
- "You're doing the right thing to abort."
- "Abortion is perfectly safe."
- "Abortion is no big deal."
- "Abortion is a legal right."
- "You have no other choice."
- "If it's legal, how can it be wrong?"
- "You're just not ready for children."
- "It's the socially responsible thing to do."
- "You can always have children later."

Because the voices who say those things are so loud and prevalent, we are made to feel ashamed that we feel differently and we are cowed into silence and stripped of our voice.

Question: To what extent do you feel you lost your voice in connection with your abortion experience? (Please circle your response.)

Not at all   Perhaps a little   More than a little   To a great extent

HOW WE GAIN BACK OUR VOICE

To gain back our voice, we need to address each of the three ways above that may have left us voiceless.

First, there is a universal principle that helps us here: *Hiding our shame magnifies it and prolongs our agony. But when we reveal and renounce our shame, we find forgiveness and healing.* When we take the initiative to "come clean" and talk about what we did, we regain our voice.

It is said, "Confession is good for the soul." This is so true. One of the key steps for gaining back our voice and beginning our healing process is to share our abortion story with each other. We are not suggesting that you tell your story to just anyone, for not everyone will receive it well.

Many men feel that they need healing following their role in an abortion, but that feeling sometimes does not surface until many years after their abortion experience. If you are one of those men, by sharing your story in a safe, caring environment, you will probably find release and a measure of healing.

Often, *the process of remembering is the beginning of healing.* This is because you are forced to recognize exactly what you're dealing with. Denying or ignoring any pain you might be experiencing from your role in an abortion will only prolong your agony.

Coming to the point in which a man reveals the secret of his role in an abortion frees his spirit. What has been hidden is now in the open.

Now he can speak. Getting your story "out in the open" (in the context of your AbAnon group) takes away much of the power from the guilt and shame you may have been feeling.

Second, if you feel you were in some way ignored or without input in the abortion decision, you must denounce any victim mentality that remains. As long as we view ourselves as "victims" we remain powerless and voiceless. Victims always remain victims. A victim cannot rise above their circumstances.

Third, recognize that although the voice of our culture and others may be loud this does not make them right. What the media or others declare does not necessarily express what you believe or are experiencing. You know what you feel. No one can argue with your experience.

Take your voice back. Read back over this list of declarations. Take a few moments and reword each of these statements based on how you feel about your abortion role today.

- "Abortion is a good choice."
- "You're doing the right thing to abort."
- "Abortion is perfectly safe."
- Abortion is no big deal."
- Abortion is a legal right."
- "You have no other choice."
- "If it's legal, how can it be wrong?"
- "You're just not ready for children."
- "It's the socially responsible thing to do."
- "You can always have children later."

By telling your story, you give validity to the fact that your abortion experience significantly impacted your life. This is very important when so many are telling you to slough it off and forget about it. Others may say, "It's no big deal," but if it has been troubling to you, then sharing your story will validate what you've been feeling.

SHARING YOUR STORY

There are also several other reasons to share your abortion story—especially in the context of a safe, caring environment like we seek to provide in your AbAnon small group.

First, hearing other men's stories may encourage you that you're not alone. There are many other men who have experienced similar things. They understand what you're going through. They can empathize with you. They've experienced things like: confusion, inner turmoil, shame, guilt, grief, or pain.

Second, as you hear others' stories, you may realize things that you hadn't thought of before. Hearing their experiences may help you identify past (and perhaps present) behaviors that may be harmful.

Third, hearing other men's stories will no doubt evoke compassion in you and allow you to extend grace and understanding toward them and receive it yourself. While being transparent and gracious with each other, we learn to be gracious in our other relationships as well.

Fourth, sharing your story with this small group of men will hopefully help you bond with them and deepen your relationships with them.

Finally, as you share your story and hear the other men in the group tell their stories, you will experience the power of standing together. We were never meant to try to struggle through life alone. We need each other. Take advantage of this tremendous support system being made available to you.

TAKE ACTION: PASS SELF-ASSESSMENT AND WRITE YOUR STORY

PASS Self-Assesment

Take a few moments and go over the two PASS lists in the material on pages 33-35. Of course, many of these PASS symptoms apply specifically to women, but many of them apply to men as well. Of the symptoms that apply to men, check those that you have experienced in the past or are experiencing now. This exercise is for your eyes only, so please be completely honest with yourself.

It's important for us to recognize that these lists represent *symptoms* of a root issue and not the issue itself.

Write Your Story

Below are some questions you may want to consider when writing your story. We encourage you to write a story for each abortion experience you have had.

1. How old were you when you were involved in the abortion?

2. What factors led to your abortion?

3. Describe the relationship you were in that led to the pregnancy?

4. What were your goals and aspirations at that time?

5. Who made the decision to abort your child?

6. What role did you play in the actual abortion procedure?

7. If involved, what do you remember about the abortion procedure itself?

8. How did you feel immediately following the abortion procedure or immediately following your learning about the abortion?

9. Where did you go? What did you do?
   Who were you with?

10. In what ways has the abortion affected your life since it occurred?

11. What else would be helpful for you to either get off your chest or share for someone else's benefit?

SESSION THREE

BILL'S STORY

Please read the following true story and reflect on the questions that follow.

Key to my story and unique from the stories of so many other men who were involved in an abortion is the fact that I was adopted. I learned that I was adopted around the age of eight or nine and throughout my adolescent years I never quite felt like I fit in. This "outsider" feeling was of my own doing; my adoptive parents loved me and treated me as if I was their own. I had a sister who also was adopted and she had absolutely no issue with it. She knew that I felt like an outsider and regularly used my condition as a means to tease and embarrass me.

In my later teens I eventually got over the outsider feelings and grew to become what I would consider normal. But knowing that I was adopted and that adoption is a viable choice for those facing an unplanned pregnancy makes my involvement in an abortion even more painful.

During my sophomore year at the University of Montana I became a Christian with the encouragement of some friends connected with

Campus Crusade for Christ (now called CRU). The following year, I met a beautiful, vivacious girl who would eventually become my wife. I was a junior; she was a freshman and a Christian as well. We were as much in love as any two people could possibly be.

She was from Billings, Montana where her parents were prominent in their community. Her father was a retired lieutenant colonel in the Marine Corps and had worked at the Pentagon.

We became engaged around Thanksgiving of my senior year but similar to the feelings of my youth, I felt like I didn't fit in or measure up to her parents' expectations for their little girl.

Two months after our engagement we learned that she was pregnant. She was convinced that we had to abort the child, "My parents will absolutely disown us if they find out we became pregnant before marriage." So we aborted our child. I did not want the abortion and we fought about it for several weeks. I didn't fight hard enough…

I will never forget that day. I managed to get enough money to pay for the abortion and went with her to the clinic. I held her hand throughout the procedure. I can vividly remember the scraping and the suction. The suction hose was clear plastic and I could see body parts as they passed through. After the abortion we had a sense of relief, her fears of her parents' disapproval were gone. But with our sense of relief also came a deep sense of loss.

We got married that summer. She went on to complete her elementary teaching degree while I worked several jobs to pay the bills. After unsuccessfully searching for a teaching position, she took a job working in retail while I continued to work three jobs. I convinced myself that this was what we needed to do to get ahead; I was still trying to measure up to her parents' expectations. She needed me at home, but I was working too much. We started drifting apart and fighting over little things.

We realized that our marriage needed help and we agreed to go to see our pastor for marriage counseling. During our third counseling appointment I was informed that, after just three and a half years of marriage, she was filing for divorce.

I was totally blindsided. She immediately moved out of the home we had just purchased and I was left wondering what had just happened. I begged her not to divorce and tried to reach out to her many times. I remember her parents telling me on one such occasion to "get over it and get on with your life."

The abortion had deeply affected her. She needed me to comfort and care for her, but at that time I just didn't see it. I knew that she had been hanging out at a local bar after work with a female co-worker but later learned that she had been having at least one affair. I still loved her. I knew that I was just as much at fault and wanted to reconcile, but to no avail.

A couple of years later, the morning following Super Bowl Sunday in 1988, I received a phone call that my ex-wife was dead. Sitting in her car in her parents' closed garage, engine running, she had ended her life. I later learned that she had just had a fight with her mom and that she was once again pregnant while unmarried.

After my divorce I was in and out of a couple of relationships, and about five years later was remarried. I had walked away from the Faith I had found in college. In my desire to be healed from the wounds caused by the divorce and death of my first wife I eventually returned to church. I found that healing with the help of John Eldredge's book Wild at Heart. It seemed as though he had written that book just for me.

My first wife and I had never talked about our abortion – the pain was so great that neither of us wanted to bring it up. I don't know whether she ever told her parents about the abortion, but my guess is that she never did. No one knew her better than I and I can tell you with complete certainty that she killed herself out of overwhelming guilt over her abortion.

I said earlier that I was adopted, but what I didn't tell you was that I was conceived when my biological mother was raped. My biological mother had every socially acceptable justification to terminate my life, yet she chose to endure the shame and the pain that went along with bringing me into this world. My personal guilt for my involvement in the abortion of my child is greatly magnified when I consider my personal history and that I too could easily have been aborted had it not been for the choice of a courageous woman.

The life of my first wife came to a tragic end, but only by the grace of God was I able to find forgiveness and freedom from the spirit of despair that settled on both of us on that horrible day.

—Bill 2015

DISCUSS BILL'S STORY

1. In what ways can you identify with Bill's story? What were you feeling?

2. What did Bill do to process his role in an abortion?

3. What can you take away from Bill's story that may help you heal?

TAKING STOCK

Hampton Morgan is man who helps men identify areas in their lives in which they struggle. He then assists them in making whatever corrections are necessary to move forward with a life that is healthy and productive. In his book, *Choosing Integrity: The Structure of Character*, Hampton makes a series of statements which he then uses when working with men.

This "taking stock" process includes fifteen statements, each followed by these word choices: Strongly Agree, Agree, Not Sure, Disagree and Strongly Disagree. With Hampton's permission we have borrowed these fifteen statements and you will see these fifteen statements again in session eight. We are asking you to use them to "take stock" of your life as well by circling the response that most closely fits you. Here are the fifteen statements:

1. I have made more than my share of impulsive decisions that I later regretted making.

    Strongly Agree   Agree   Not Sure   Disagree   Strongly Disagree

2. I have usually had the self-control I needed to keep me from doing things I later regret.

    Strongly Agree   Agree   Not Sure   Disagree   Strongly Disagree

3. I stay angry longer than I think is healthy for me.

    Strongly Agree   Agree   Not Sure   Disagree   Strongly Disagree

4. I have forgiven the people who have done the most harm to me.

    Strongly Agree   Agree   Not Sure   Disagree   Strongly Disagree

5. I struggle with addictive substances.

    Strongly Agree   Agree   Not Sure   Disagree   Strongly Disagree

6. I struggle with addictive behaviors.

    Strongly Agree   Agree   Not Sure   Disagree   Strongly Disagree

7. I have achieved the goals I expected to reach by this point in my life.

    Strongly Agree   Agree   Not Sure   Disagree   Strongly Disagree

8. I feel hopeful about the future.

    Strongly Agree   Agree   Not Sure   Disagree   Strongly Disagree

9. I have at least one trusted and reliable friend I can turn to in time of need.

    Strongly Agree   Agree   Not Sure   Disagree   Strongly Disagree

10. I take responsibility for being where I am today, and I do not blame anyone else.

   Strongly Agree   Agree   Not Sure   Disagree   Strongly Disagree

11. I have suffered serious trauma in my life and feel I have not really gotten over it.

   Strongly Agree   Agree   Not Sure   Disagree   Strongly Disagree

12. I wish I had a deeper spiritual life or connection with God.

   Strongly Agree   Agree   Not Sure   Disagree   Strongly Disagree

13. I feel like I keep making the same mistakes and bad decisions again and again.

   Strongly Agree   Agree   Not Sure   Disagree   Strongly Disagree

14. I have a strong sense of right and wrong that I think most people would agree with.

   Strongly Agree   Agree   Not Sure   Disagree   Strongly Disagree

15. I have had an experience in my life that still causes me to feel shame when I think about it.

   Strongly Agree   Agree   Not Sure   Disagree   Strongly Disagree

As you ponder your responses to the statements listed above, which statements, if any, trigger feelings of DESPAIR? The Beast of Despair comes on post-abortive men in two very different ways; feeling emasculated or feeling trapped.

FOR MANY, ABORTION MEANT FEELING EMASCULATED

At the time of this writing, 2016, there has been growing sentiment that men should have some say in what happens with the child they have fathered. This notion is growing in popularity, but many believe legalized abortion will end BEFORE men ever have a legal voice in the matter.

Not only do men have no *legal* say in the abortion decision, often they are silenced or completely left out of any discussion. This is especially true if the father was very young or the father wanted to keep the child.

Unfortunately, it is true that the child's father is often the source of pressure to abort. But the results of a study, led by Dr. Priscilla Coleman of Bowling State University and published in the 2010 *Journal of Pregnancy,* found that nearly 48 percent of women who underwent late abortions and 30 percent of women who had early abortions said that they were pressured to abort by someone other than their partner.

In hearing men's stories where the decision to abort was made without their input or over their objections, men commonly describe themselves as feeling emasculated, powerless or helpless. No doubt many men feel it unfair or unjust that their child was aborted without their wishes being considered. In many cases this has led to despair. They believe that the child was just as much theirs as the mother's. Many believe that they had the responsibility to protect their child, but were denied their right to do so. They feel emasculated and fall into despair as a result.

FOR MANY, ABORTION MEANT FEELING TRAPPED

Despair is also a common emotion in cases where the father of the aborted child indeed had input or voice in the decision but because of the circumstances surrounding the situation he felt trapped and that there was no other way out. So ultimately it came down to the desperate choice of destroying his life or the life of a nameless, genderless, faceless child.

Frederica Mathewes-Green of Feminists for Life of America describes the despair that many women feel when deciding to abort, but the same can be said for many situations that men find themselves. "No woman wants an abortion as she wants an ice cream or a Porsche. She wants an abortion as an animal caught in a trap wants to gnaw off its own leg."[26]

In such a case, the decision to abort is fraught with despair. Her maternal instincts and hormones have already begun to influence her physically and emotionally. But she's torn because she sees this unexpected pregnancy as the end of all she's planned and hoped for. She desperately wants things back "the way they were."

While men will never experience the physical influence of abortion, the emotional influence can be just as severe. A man's instinct to protect the child and the woman are silenced by the abortion.

Couples may *agonize* over the decision whether to have an abortion. The fact that their collective consciences are active and tormenting them over their decision may lead them to rationalize that the pain of the struggle itself makes it morally acceptable.

However, most people who are involved in abortions do so believing it is morally wrong.[27] But at this point, in despair and hopelessness,

---

26   Frederica Mathewes-Green, *Real Choices* (Sisters, OR: Multnomah Books, 1994), p. 19.
27   Over 70% of women who abort, do so against their conscience. David C. Reardon, PhD, p. 191.

many people capitulate—defying their conscience and values. In a state of shock they numbly go through the motions of the abortion. Often, even while lying on the operating table or holding their partner's hand while standing there in support, they are screaming inside, "My God, what am I doing!"

But it's too late. The deed is now done. And the despair that drove them to abort is by no means gone! Oh, they may feel relief at first; most couples do. But months or years later, the despair, like an angry ravenous beast, has now feasted on the abortion and rises to greater strength to consume each of them as well.

THE BEAST OF DESPAIR

Whether it was through emasculation or being trapped, this beast of despair now snarls at many men, "You are such a worthless person! Look at what you failed to do, allowing your child to be taken! You are good for nothing and fit for no one!" Or the beast may taunt other men, "You are such a horrible person! Look what you've done, taking the life of your child! You are worthless, good for nothing and fit for no one!"

In his despair, the man believes the accusations and slandering of this beast. He believes he is unworthy of love. He thinks, "God could never forgive me. I acted cowardly and put my needs above those whom I had a duty to protect. God will never trust me with children again. I don't deserve anything good." And he begins living out this desperate life that he now envisions for himself.

He may try to medicate himself with drugs, alcohol, porn, or unbridled sexual escapades. Or he may try to stuff his despair by burying himself in a career or some extreme hobby— anything to take his mind off of the abortion and his despair. Sometimes men become self-destructive, contemplating suicide and even attempting it. Other men fall into patterns of angry outbursts, especially toward those they love. Any of these efforts will only intensify despair, increasing its downward spiral.

In fear and anguish, the man now reflects on his own shortcomings or upon those who emasculated him and left him powerless. He despises them. He despises himself.

All of this may be very painful for some who are reading this. If *despair* led you to abort, or if *despair* is what your felt because of being powerless, then *despair* will prevent you from healing. The question is how do we replace despair with hope?

REPLACING DESPAIR WITH HOPE

If either of the above situations describes you, there are at least four things you can do to destroy this beast of despair in your life. **First**, recognize that the accusations of this beast are false. They are lies. Even though you may now believe your abortion was wrong, the abortion does not diminish your worth as a person, or as a man. Your worth is not measured by what you've done or haven't done, but by who you are. You are a valuable person, a person of magnificent potential to help others.

Second, identify and reject self-destructive behaviors. You cannot "pay" for what you did or what you allowed to happen to your child. Your child would not want you hurt. Harming yourself in any way will only bring you and those you love more misery, hopelessness and pain. Instead, seek those habits, behaviors and thoughts that are wholesome, healthy and promote hope.

A great way to instill hope is to provide hope to others by serving them. Perhaps you could look for ways to help other post-abortive men; volunteer at a charity; or help the homeless. Serving others may seem like the last thing you'd want to do right now. But experience shows that serving others is very therapeutic. Build your life around positive, healthy people and practices.

Third, strive to let go of anger and bitterness and seek to forgive others. When an animal is injured in the wild, it often crawls off to die alone. Because we feel wounded, we may be tempted to do the same. Being angry and bitter toward others fuels our imagination with evil thoughts about them and drives us into isolation and loneliness. We'll talk more about relationships and forgiveness in a later chapter.

Fourth, draw near to others who love you deeply—in spite of your abortion. Their love substantiates that you are lovable. You were created to love and to be loved. You are worthy of good and capable of wonderful things. Accept their love and let it fill you with hope for a brighter future.

TAKE ACTION

Look back over those four ways of replacing despair with hope mentioned above. Which ones will you begin to put into practice this week? How will you do that?

_____

_____

_____

_____

_____

_____

_____

Go somewhere quiet and alone. Hold a mirror up to your face. Look beyond the reflection you see in the mirror and identify at least 10 positive attributes about yourself. List these positive attributes here and state them in this fashion: "I am: ..."

a._____

b._____

c._____

d._____

e._____

f._____

g._____

h._____

i._____

j._____

SESSION FOUR

JERRY'S STORY

Please read the following true story and reflect on the questions that follow.

My girlfriend and I had been living together for two or three years. We were heavily engaged in a party lifestyle including drugs, alcohol and sexual involvement with another couple. Consequently, when my girl-friend got pregnant, we didn't know for sure who the father was.

Besides the fact that a baby would've cramped our party style, not knowing whose it was played a major role in our decision to get an abortion. The abortion was a mutual decision. My girlfriend was very pro-women's rights, so she saw the abortion as her prerogative and I was in full agreement.

I accompanied her to the abortion clinic and stayed with her during the procedure. It was a horrible experience. She was very upset and cried through the whole thing. I was helpless to do anything for her.

In the days following the abortion, both of us experienced mild depres-sion—certainly she did more than I. Then we tried to move on from the abortion. We didn't really go through a grieving process at the time, nor did we talk about the abortion. But as time went on, we often wondered, "What if we had kept the baby?"

Meanwhile, we continued living our party lifestyle. We had been living together for five years when we decided to get married. After our wedding, we decided to have kids and that decision took our minds back to the abortion. I think that's when it first hit us that we had aborted a person and we began wondering a lot more about the baby we had aborted.

During those next months, my wife had two miscarriages and we couldn't help but wonder if they resulted from the abortion. Finally, she was able to carry a baby and our boy was born. After the birth of our son, I went into a 12-step recovery program to get off drugs and alcohol. My feelings started changing and I began thinking about God.

The 12 Steps caused me to look back in my past and ask forgiveness from people I had hurt and to make amends. During this time, both my wife and I turned to Christ. We put our trust in Him for forgiveness of our sins and chose to follow Him.

My wife hesitantly decided to attend a post-abortive recovery group. As she did, my sensitivity toward our abortion and abortion in general heightened. We both really began feeling remorse over our abortion. I wept bitterly over what we'd done.

Not until then, did I think back to a girl I had gotten pregnant at camp when I was in high school. We had lived in different towns and she contacted me after camp telling me she was pregnant. It was easy to just send her money and let her take care of her "problem."

But now, with my new perspective on abortion, I looked her up, called her and asked her to forgive me. She wasn't ready for that and was angry with me for suggesting that it had been wrong.

Today, I still deal with regret over my abortions. There are so many reminders—seeing a child, a TV commercial, or a billboard—brings it all back. I wonder what could've been had we let my two children live. I know that I have God's forgiveness, but the regret never goes away.

After our boy was born, my wife had an ectopic pregnancy (outside the uterus) and had to have major surgery to save her life. In all, she was pregnant five times, but we only have the one child to show for it. The abortion affected her profoundly both emotionally and physically and I still grieve and feel sad over it.

Today, I am very grateful to God for our son! He's an amazing young man. He's about to graduate from high school with honors and earned a full scholarship to a private college. We're very proud of him. I thank Jesus Christ for His abundant forgiveness and grace in our lives! In spite of our mistakes and sins, He loves us and has given us so much!

—Jerry 2015

DISCUSS JERRY'S STORY

1. In what ways can you identify with Jerry's story? What were you feeling?

2. What did Jerry do to process his role in an abortion?

3. What can you take away from Jerry's story that may help you heal?

REGRET AND YOUR BABY

Regret is another emotion that many men manifest to express the *pain* of their involvement in an abortion. We all have past regrets. Regret is sorrow over things we've done that we wish we hadn't; and things we didn't do, but wish we had.

Men commonly express a number of regrets around their abortion. Look at the list that follows and check all that apply to you.

I regret that…

☐ I was even dating that girl/woman.

☐ I had sex with her at the time.

☐ I got her pregnant in the first place.

☐ We listened to those who urged us to get the abortion.

☐ We didn't listen to those who tried to dissuade us from having the abortion.

☐ Our friends, parents, siblings or someone else close
didn't keep us from aborting our child.

☐ I had anything to do with having the abortion.

☐ I couldn't do anything to prevent my child from being
aborted.

☐ I don't know my child, its gender, or anything else about
him/her.

☐ Other:_____

_____

_____

_____

Much like the other emotions many men feel as a result of their role in an abortion, regret prevents us from moving past our grief. One reason that regret is so debilitating is that it is based on something that happened in the *past*. The problem is we cannot change the past. So, to continually live in regret over our past abortion is futile—and cannot help us get beyond it.

We carry regret around like too much baggage. This baggage encumbers us and weighs us down. No matter where we go, we find ourselves dragging this heavy load with us. Sometimes the emotional strain we feel under this burden is unbearable. Yet we feel torn. On the one hand, we wish we could discard this great burden, and on the other hand we feel that we dare not part with it.

So it is with the regrets around our role in an abortion. We feel terrible about our abortion and know that we must never deny the gravity of what we've done. But we wish we could somehow shed some of its weight. Consequently, in some measure there will always be feelings of regret.

But too much regret can weigh us down, crushing us under its weight and making life a constant struggle.

We experience waves of remorse, sorrow, and grief over what we've done *and* what was done to us. We have an unquenchable longing to somehow miraculously undo what was done—*but we can't*. At times we may get caught in the whirlpool of "What ifs" around the whole abortion experience. But going there only stirs up *more* regret.

The regret we feel is often tied directly to our child. Before the abortion, our culture and others around us may have led us to think about our child in the following terms:

- Depersonalized
- Dehumanized ("It's just tissue")
- Removed or distant
- Surreal, or unreal
- But at some time after our abortion we may experience:
- Reality set in about our child—it was a human being, a person
- We desire to know about our child—its gender, hair and eye color, etc.
- We may fantasize about our child and what he or she would have been like

As we mentioned, regret, sorrow and grief are all forms of emotional pain. As with physical pain, pain plays an important role in letting us know "something is wrong." As such, there are only two primary responses to pain: we can either suppress it, or take steps to cope with it.

While suppressing the pain may be a coping mechanism, it's not a good one, because it doesn't solve anything. Suppressing or ignoring regret and sorrow, though common, is an irrational response that will result in abnormal behaviors leading to more regret.

Instead, we must take steps toward coping effectively with our regret. We offer three steps here, but you may discover other steps as well.

1. **Lay down the baggage of "what ifs" and second guessing.** You cannot change the past no matter how badly you wish you could. Settle that in your mind and unload that burden from your shoulders.

    "God grant me the serenity to accept the things I cannot change, the courage to change the things I can, and the wisdom to know the difference." — Reinhold Niebuhr

2. **Discard the baggage of things you could not control.** No doubt there were circumstances around your abortion over which you had no control. If so, you are carrying someone else's baggage. Release it and be free from it.

3. **Set down that trunk full of old tapes that you carry around with you and keep replaying.** You know the tapes that I'm referring to: they are reruns of your whole abortion experience. These may include conversations, people you'd rather forget, driving your girlfriend to the cold clinic, the noises and smells. Shut them all tight in that trunk and push it off the end of a dock into the depths of the ocean. Be done with it.

Yes, there will always be a reasonable amount of regret attached to your role in the abortion, but learn to travel light when it comes to regret.

TAKE ACTION

Please take time to get alone and walk through those three steps for coping with regret. Visualize yourself laying down the weighty burden of each one. Take your time. Make sure you really do put it down and walk away from it. Record here for future reference what you did with each of these burdens.

1. Lay down the baggage of "what ifs" and second-guessing.

2. Discard the baggage of things you could not control. Rid yourself of the burden of someone else's baggage.

3. Set down that trunk full of old tapes that you carry around with you and keep replaying. Then push that trunk off the end of a dock into the deep ocean

Finally, is there another heavy piece of baggage that we did not identify that you can also lay down? If so, write that down here and take steps to abandon it like the others.

SESSION FIVE

TERRY'S STORY

Please read the following true story and reflect on the questions that follow.

My story is one I believe that possibly millions of men can relate to. I grew up in a middle-class family; my father had served in the military and provided for our family by working a blue-collar job most of his working years. I was the youngest of four children including a much older half-sister from my mother's first marriage. My parents taught us the value of giving back to our community, themselves being foster parents for a dozen or so children throughout the years, and even adopting a fifth child when I was in my teens.

Like any family, we were far from perfect, but I think people viewed our family as "good people." We attended church semi-regularly and I was baptized as a child. My moral compass may not have been set on true north but it was pointing generally in the right direction.

As I grew out of my teenage years and into my twenties, I gradually moved away from what I knew in my heart to be right. Basically what I was taught as a child was not strong enough to suppress my raging hormones, a common malady with young men.

In my mid-twenties I began a career in Fire Service and met a gal during EMT training. After dating a few months we moved in together; she was a few years older than me and brought a six-year-old son and a nine-year-old daughter into the relationship. Our relationship was not a strong one; it lacked commitment on my part. For me our relationship was one of convenience, I provided her the emotional and child-rearing support she needed and she provided what I needed.

After living together for about a year she discovered that she was pregnant and informed me that she had made the decision to abort the child. Who could blame her? She already had two kids and was in the physical testing phase as she prepared for a job in public protective services. But I think the true reason for her aborting our child was that she felt trapped – no way out – she was pregnant with a third child and I didn't offer any support or encouragement of any kind. In other words, she had no confidence in our relationship and I said nothing, neglecting my God-given duty to take responsibility for my actions and to be the protector of my family.

After the abortion I remember feeling guilty about it…I knew that what we had done was wrong. I say "we" because deep within my soul, even though it was her decision, I failed to stop it when I had the power to do so.

A year later and newly hired at a job she had spent years training for, she was pregnant again. Unfortunately nothing had changed within me or within our relationship. This time we both decided to abort the child. The guilt I was carrying was not yet bad enough to change my behavior.

After the second abortion I couldn't stand it any longer… I wanted out and I told her so. She was devastated. She tried to kill herself by taking a lethal dose of very powerful medication. Thanks to my medical training I recognized what was happening and rushed her to the ER in the middle of the night; only minutes away from dying the team at the ER got her through it.

We never talked about it, but I can't help but think that the two abortions had something to do with her mental state and they certainly affected mine. I attempted to break up again, but this attempt also failed. Looking back maybe I should have just walked away, but I couldn't just leave her after all we'd been through. However I did take off for a month, basically I had to get away for a while. During that month I was constantly stoned or drunk.

Eventually we parted ways and each of us moved on with our lives.

Around age thirty-eight I started attending church again in an attempt to fill the huge hole in my heart. I can't say that I've ever had one of those "God encounters" but several friends and Pastors have prayed with me, asking God to forgive me for my role in these abortions and for many other things I've done. I'm still a work in progress but I know that my moral compass is once again generally pointing in the right direction.

I don't think about my involvement with the two abortions every day. I know that I'm forgiven, but those abortions still sit at the top of the heap of my own condemnation. In retrospect, I wonder how I could ever have gotten to the point where my own selfishness had caused me to lose my spiritual, emotional and physiological perspective to the point where I was willing to kill my own children.

As a paramedic I'm in the life-saving business. I know what I did and there is no intellectually honest way to rationalize it. Except for my daughter from a marriage years later, there is nothing that I wouldn't give to go back and change what I've done. And I hope that by telling my story I may be able to save others from suffering from the same regret and shame as I have.

—Terry, 2015

DISCUSS TERRY'S STORY

1. In what ways can you identify with Terry's story? What were you feeling?

2. What did Terry do to process his role in an abortion?

3. What can you take away from Terry's story that may help you heal?

ANGER

Anger is a very personal emotional response that exhibits frustration and agitation over a situation that we can no longer change. Anger usually focuses on what is past—on something that already happened. Anger displays antagonism toward others over hurt or frustration that we are feeling, whether those individuals have anything to do with our hurt and frustration or not.

Many men respond to their role in an abortion with anger. In many cases, we may not even know why we're angry. Perhaps we've never even associated our anger with our involvement in an abortion or in the role we played.

As men who have participated to some degree in an abortion, we often feel angry at ourselves, at those who ignored us while having an abortion, at others who participated in some other way, and at those who failed to intervene and provide a way out. We may also be angry at the circumstances leading up to and resulting from our role in the abortion. Often, we may be angry with God for allowing this to happen, even though we must admit our part in it.

Of all the emotions we feel, anger is one of the most dangerous and volatile. Anger is a desperate attempt to regain control over a situation in which we feel we've lost control. As a result, we lash out at ourselves or others. Anger provokes irrational and unhealthy thoughts, words, and behavior.

Anger is also very contagious and destroys relationships. For example, in our anger over our role in an abortion, we may lash out at a loved one who just happens to be nearby. Perhaps we don't feel *worthy* of love, so why should this person love us? In our anger, we push them away rejecting their love and denying them ours.

Anger often causes us to do things contrary to our conscience and moral standards. Anger can lead to self-destructive behaviors like: drinking, drugs, sexual escapades, binge eating, unrestrained gambling, pornography and all sorts of other behaviors that only worsen our situation. In cases of self-abuse, we subconsciously direct our anger toward ourselves as punishment for what we've done or failed to do.

Anger is an emotion that we *yield* to. We feel justified in being angry. We give anger free reign and let it dictate our responses to life. This is scary. When anger is in control, we cannot heal and we injure others. Anger is like acid that eats away at the person holding it.[28]

The awful things we think and say about ourselves become self-fulfilling prophecies.

Anger, if unrestrained, consumes our life. Anger weaves strong patterns in our lives that are difficult to break. We're angry over our abortion and we look for things around us to justify and feed our anger. For this reason, we must recognize that the thing we're angry at in the moment may not be the source or root of our anger—our abortion.

---

28   Based on Mark Twain's quote, "Anger is an acid that can do more harm to the vessel in which it is stored than to anything on which it is poured."

Over time, various responses to our abortion may include: *hiding, denying, blaming,* and *rationalizing* or *justifying.* Anger may be a common emotion for us in any and all of these responses.

HOW DO WE GET RID OF ANGER?

In order to break the patterns of anger in our lives, we must identify its root cause. Anger is a very *relational* response. What that means is that even if we are angry over a situation or an event, we invariably direct our anger toward *people.* This may be ourselves, God, anyone else who was involved in our abortion, or we may take out our anger on those around us who have nothing to do with our abortion. Anger expresses itself toward people.

Because of this relational aspect of anger, the only way to truly rid ourselves of anger is to forgive those who have offended us—including ourselves. When we're angry at someone, we put the onus on them to change, not realizing that *we* need to change. *We* must take the initiative. *Forgiveness is vital, because it removes the reason for our anger.* For some of us, forgiving others and ourselves may be extremely difficult.

First, we may think that if we forgive someone for their role in the pregnancy or the abortion that we are somehow condoning their actions. This is not true. In reality, the act of forgiveness *validates* that there is a real offense which warrants forgiving.

Second, we mistakenly think that by withholding forgiveness from someone, we exercise control over them. We may think that by not forgiving them, we continue to hold something over them. This is a form of revenge. The irony is that withholding forgiveness from others harms *us* more than it harms them. Someone has wisely said, "Refusal to forgive someone is like drinking poison and hoping the other person suffers."

Finally, forgiveness is often difficult for us because we have held onto anger for so long it has become a part of us. Anger has woven its patterns into our life. We may even feel that parting with our anger will strip us of something dear to us. This thinking is part of the folly of anger. It is irrational and controls us. It's like keeping a rabid dog in the basement that we continue to feed, even though we're afraid of it. But we will only find relief when we remove the cause of our anger.

We cannot go back and erase our abortion, but we can forgive others and ourselves for our role in it. Doing so will help us end the awful rule of anger in our lives.

TAKE ACTION: STEPS TO FORGIVING OTHERS

1. **Identify those with whom you are angry.** Write down here everyone who was also involved or shared any role with you in your abortion experience and toward whom you may be directing anger. (Include anyone and everyone that even remotely had a role in the abortion, including yourself.)

2. **Forgive each of these individuals.** We are not suggesting that you actually go to each of these individuals or even call or write them. (In some cases, you may choose to do so, but not for everyone.) There are two parts to this step:

   a. **Prepare a short statement that you will actually speak aloud.** This statement may say something like: "(person's name), I forgive you for your role in that abortion experience and I release my grudge against you."

b. **Speak these words of forgiveness for each person on your list.** Go somewhere private to do this. Work through your list and speak your statement of forgiveness aloud in your own hearing. Saying it aloud is important because it helps validate the act and demands that you speak it in a way that you mean it.

3. **Next, understand that anger is a two-way street.** People have offended us and therefore we are angry. Remember, as long as we hold onto anger it controls and poisons us. Forgiving others is the key to freedom from anger.

    But *we* have offended others as well (through our role in aborting our child, or by the way we've treated them). So too, if we have offended others, we can find refreshment and freedom by going to them and asking their forgiveness. By taking initiative to ask their forgiveness, we also offer them freedom from their anger.

    You must approach this step using some common sense:

    a. **Make this a short list.** Who are the people that really matter in your life? Have you offended them? If so, go to them and ask them to forgive you. As I write this, I know a woman who aborted her child without the father's knowledge. He was very hurt by her act and now she deeply regrets her abortion as well. She needs his forgiveness and he needs to forgive her.

    b. **Choose your words wisely.** Words like, "Sorry if I offended you," can sound insincere and hypocritical. Say something like, "I'm sorry I offended you. Would you please forgive me?" If you feel you need to provide the person with the context for your apology, then do so.

4. **Consider asking God to forgive you.** As you read this, you will know whether this step is right for you now. If you would like to ask God's forgiveness for your role in an abortion and other actions that have followed as a result, simply talk to Him and tell Him you're sorry and ask Him to forgive you. God loves it when we come to Him like this. He will not turn you away or deny you forgiveness.

5. **Be prepared for reappearances of anger.** Because anger may have been your companion for many years, it will try to come back and take hold of you again. That's why it's important to record above what you have done: whom you've forgiven and what you said. Then, when anger does raise its ugly head again, come back to what you did in this exercise. You may need to do this from time to time. Some people experience an immediate and complete sense of release and freedom in forgiveness. With others it occurs over time. If you're one of those who continues to struggle with anger and forgiveness, don't be discouraged or frustrated, but keep at it. Come back to actions you initiated in this exercise. Keep rehearsing the truth of what you know.

SESSION SIX

RON'S STORY

Please read the following true story and reflect on the questions that follow.

My girlfriend and I were both 16 and in high school when we started dating. She was my first real girlfriend.

My parents were divorced and my dad had remarried right away and started a new family. He simply walked away from my mom, my sister and me and completely left our lives. My mom had a boyfriend, who moved in with us, but he was very weird and I didn't want to be around him. He lost his job shortly after moving in, so my mom went to work and he hung around the house all day.

Consequently, I had no good role model or instruction from a father or father figure in my life. My sister got pregnant when she was just 14 or 15. She had a baby girl; brought her home, and then my sister ran away, leaving her child for my mom to care for. My mom really loved her granddaughter.

My sister eventually returned home and decided to give her little girl up for adoption. My sister did not have a good relationship with my mom and she put her baby up for adoption to hurt my mom. It was all quite a mess.

Meanwhile, I spent a lot of time at my girlfriend's house. I was drawn into her family. Her parents went sailing a lot in the summer and invited me to come along. I liked being included in her family.

My girlfriend and I started having sex and she called me one day and told me she thought she was pregnant. I wasn't prepared for that at all. She and I went together to a clinic to confirm her pregnancy. I asked her, "What are we going to do?" We were so young and naïve.

A week went by and she told me she wanted to have an abortion. She simply announced that this is what she was going to do. She didn't want to deal with the embarrassment and responsibility of a child as a 16-year-old. Although I had not thought of abortion, it seemed the easy way out of our problem.

She asked me to figure out how to pay for the abortion, so I sold my car stereo to get the money. Neither of us said anything to her parents or my mom.

I took my girlfriend to the procedure and stayed at her side through the whole ordeal. It was awful! The procedure was terrible, gruesome and very traumatic for her. We weren't at all prepared for how devastating the abortion would be.

Immediately following the abortion, she began distancing herself from me. We stopped having sex. After the abortion, sex seemed dirty to me.

Right away I began feeling remorse and guilt. Even though I had absolutely zero religious upbringing, I had sensed deep down inside that abortion was wrong. Now we were both experiencing the consequences for our action.

I reasoned now that if we had had the child I would have taken care of it. Both of us began wondering whether our child had been a boy or girl and what he/she would have looked like. It was very distressing.

In my heart, I felt the baby had been a boy. Even today, so many years later I think about him a lot, wondering where he would have been today. Would he be married now with kids of his own?

My girlfriend and I had no one to talk to. We dare not tell her parents and I didn't tell my mom until five years later. I kick myself for doing nothing to talk my girlfriend out of the abortion. I now believe that she was upset with me for not manning up and showing her another way out.

But I was selfish and fulfilled my wants instead of my child's. I deeply regret what I did. I felt tremendous shame and held myself back from others thinking that surely they must know what I had done.

The abortion deeply impacted my life. My girlfriend and I drifted apart. I eventually met someone else and married her. But the abortion affected me starting a family. I felt so unworthy to father a child. And the abortion continued to eat away at me…I longed for a real father with whom I could talk.

When I married my first wife, I didn't marry so much out of love for her, but for her family. She had a father and a mother. They were an intact family, something I longed for. Her dad became a mentor and confidant to me. He led me into a relationship with Jesus Christ and through the forgiveness that Jesus offers I began to experience healing from the abortion.

For reasons I won't go into my wife wanted a divorce. But my relationship with her parents was so strong that they invited me to come live with them while their daughter ended our marriage.

After I came to Christ and confessed the abortion to Him, I felt a huge weight lifted from me. I know I'm forgiven, but the regret of what I did still haunts me. It's something you never forget. It's a part of my life that I'm not proud of. Abortion affected my whole life and who I am as a man. It stripped me of my self-confidence.

Eventually, I met my current wife and we've enjoyed a life together raising four children. I cherish my children deeply and spend all the time with them I possibly can. I want to be the father for them that I never had.

Recently, I ran into my girlfriend at a public event. We greeted and hugged briefly. If I had known then what I know today, I would have stepped up and fought for our baby and encouraged my girlfriend that we had other viable options.

—Ron, 2015

DISCUSS RON'S STORY

1. In what ways can you identify with Ron's story? What were you feeling?

2. What did Ron do to process his role in an abortion?

3. What can you take away from Ron's story that may help you heal?

FEAR

Whereas anger focuses on what is past, fear is anxious about what *could* happen in the future. Like anger, fear is an emotion to which we relinquish power. When we yield to fear, we grant it permission to rule over us and control us. Fear may have caused us to hide, deny, or blame someone else for our abortion.

Fear can be crippling and paralyzing. Fear can prevent us from making good decisions or making any decisions at all. To some extent, fear probably played a role in our abortion involvement. If so, our fear drove us to do something that we now deeply regret. Our role in the abortion also spawned a situation that causes us to fear in a variety of ways.

Please check any of the things below that have evoked fear in your life. As post-abortive men, we may have harbored fears about:

☐ Being found out

☐ The long-term consequences resulting from our abortion

☐ Whether people will reject us

☐ Whether God will punish us for what we did

☐ Whether God would ever trust us or allow us to have children

☐ Whether our children will repeat the same mistakes we've made

☐ Other:_____

_____

_____

_____

Lest there be any confusion, keep in mind that there are different kinds of *fear*. For instance, we can have a healthy fear of dark alleys at night that prompts us to take proper precautions. We also may cultivate a healthy fear of failure that motivates us to show up at work on time and perform our jobs well. A soldier experiences a healthy fear when going into battle and overcomes that fear with courage and training.

ANOTHER KIND OF FEAR

But the kind of fear we're talking about here is neither healthy nor overcome with safeguards. The fear we're talking about haunts and cripples us. This form of fear is unhealthy, destructive and prevents our healing. The antidote for this kind of fear is…*confidence in the love and acceptance of others that results in positive action.*

When I was a little boy, I had a very active imagination. I was convinced that when the lights went out at night, there were alligators under my bed. I'd call my dad in and ask him to remove the alligators. He'd feign a great struggle, man-handling those alligators out from underneath my bed and dragging them outside. After watching his display of courage and love, I could then fall asleep. Confident of my dad's love and with his courage as my example, my fears melted away.

While little boys have little fears, grown men can have big fears. Fear steals our joy and paralyzes us. Fear keeps us from taking risks and entering new relationships. Left unchecked, fear begins to influence our every decision. Fear can run and ruin our life.

Fear often played a role in our decision to abort our child in the first place. Now that the deed is done, we fear being found out. We fear what others might think of us. We fear the possible repercussions if this dark secret got out, While fear may be playing a harmful role or even ruining our life, many men have expressed another kind of fear that we must take a moment here to address.

No man alive wants to be thought of or labeled as a coward, but that is exactly how many men describe their role in the abortion. As harsh as it may sound there is no other way to describe how they feel; they feel that they acted *cowardly*. As men, when we realize that we acted cowardly, and whether or not anyone else knows, *we know*. It is an affront to our manhood and can eat us up on the inside. And cowardly actions in our past only accentuate our feelings of guilt, shame and fear.

In moments of personal, quiet reflection, you too may view your role in an abortion as cowardly. Maybe in your heart you know that:

- You put your fears, desires or plans above the feelings of your partner and the life of your child.

- You didn't do all you should have done to protect your child.

- You were more concerned about your reputation or what others might think than with doing what you knew to be right.

- You ran from your responsibility as a man.

In the movie, **Open Range**, Kevin Costner plays the gunslinger turned cowboy, Charlie Waite. In the saloon scene where the locals are offering excuses for not standing up to the town bully, Costner says, "You're men aren't ya? You may not know this but there are things that gnaw on a man worse than dying!"

Feelings of cowardice are one of those things that can gnaw on a man worse than dying. But what's done is done. And looking back at what's been done and allowing it to gnaw on you will serve no purpose other than to keep you in bondage to guilt and shame. Do not despair, history is loaded with stories of men who acted cowardly at first then went on to become heroes in battle, faith or social justice.

HOW DO WE STOP BEING FEARFUL?

Defeating fear or feelings of cowardice begins by being genuine and transparent and by allowing others to love who we truly are. This may feel "feminine" to some men, but everyone regardless of gender or any other qualifier desperately needs love and acceptance.

So, our fearful thoughts work like this: we assume that when people do express love and acceptance for us, our fears disqualify this as genuine. We argue that they're only loving the person that they think we are and not our true self.

We often fail to be real because we fear being rejected by others. But our fear of being rejected by others is fueled by our refusal to allow others to love us. Ironically, our fear often causes us to push them away. We may reject their love because we feel so unworthy. Or perhaps we've been burned so many times we fear being hurt again, so we withhold our love from others.

It is true, every time we love someone and allow them to love us, we run the risk of being disappointed, abandoned, or hurt. Still, even we as men desperately need the love of others in our lives. *To love and be loved is a basic human need.* When we allow fear to keep us from love, we give it permission to deny us a basic human need. As long as we're fearful, we cannot heal. And fear keeps us cowardly. Fear cripples our ability to take action and function courageously.

When we allow fear to prevent us from trusting others, we'll never experience their love—the very thing that will dispel our fear. This is one reason we discussed forgiveness last week. By forgiving others and asking their forgiveness, we have opened the door for reconciliation, trust and real love. With genuine trust and real love there can be no fear or cowardice. There is no greater love than to lay down one's life for one's friends.

In a very real way, we must deal with our irrational fears *rationally*. That is, we must face them with courage. We must decide to take a risk and allow others to love us. We must risk loving them. We must weigh this decision carefully and wisely. We don't want to abandon ourselves to someone who does not truly love us. We all know too well how poorly that will go.

A word of caution: people will pretend to love you because they want something from you. What people want from you could include money, sex, attention, security, admiration or approval.

Before exposing yourself to another person, take time to consider this question:

Would this person truly love me as I really am if I did not have
_____to offer them?

Choose wisely. There are those who do love you dearly. Abandon yourself to their love first. Let them love and comfort you and return their love freely.

TAKE ACTION: THREE STEPS FOR BECOMING FREE FROM FEAR:

1. **Make a list of people who truly love you just as you are.** These people love you unconditionally with no strings attached.

   _____

   _____

   _____

   _____

   _____

2. **From that list of people who love you, identify the person with whom you could most likely be a confidant or a friend that you could open up to and tell them anything.** This is someone you can trust, who loves you and you love them. When we talk about "love" here we are not talking about love in a romantic context. We're talking about a "best-friend" kind of love.

This person could *possibly* be your spouse, but it would be even better and much more effective if this person was another man in whom we can confide. I cannot emphasizehow important this is for your emotional, social, and spiritual health!

We must be very picky about who we choose for a confidant. Look for someone you look up to. Choose a man who doesn't necessarily have it all together, but he's also not on the brink of disaster. You're not looking for a "project" here, and neither should he.

Simply ask this person if they would start meeting with you regularly (we recommend weekly). Share the characteristics of a confidant with them below, so you're both on the same page. Commit to confidentiality and transparency. Then establish when and where you'll meet.

Be very intentional about establishing this relationship. You may already know this person, but have never thought of them as a confidant. Consider "up-grading" your current relationship. As you form this relationship, speak openly about the characteristics you would like to see in this relationship. Confidants:

a. **Spend time together in real life.** Let yourconfidant into the whole of your life. If you only see each other once a week in a coffee house, you won't really get to know each other. You have to be able to let your hair down with this person and be yourself without condemnation.

b. **Love and care for each other.** Look for ways to serve each other that will clearly demonstrate the genuineness of your love and care for each other.

c.   **Challenge each other boldly.** We are often timid about pointing out a caustic behavior in another person. But if we give each other permission to do this at the outset of our relationship, we will experience a much richer, more meaningful relationship that helps both of us grow as individuals.

d.   **Encourage each other in your spiritual journey.** Wherever you are in your journey regarding faith in God, you want someone who will move you forward rather than stifle or hinder you. Don't give up ground you've gained with God on behalf of someone else's relationship. If the other person asks for that concession, this should serve as a red flag concerning the authenticity of their love.

e.   **Celebrate one another's joys and victories.** Avoid spending time with each other merely complaining, grousing, criticizing others, or gossiping.

3.   **Seek out a healthy group of like-minded people.** These are largely lacking in our society today, but they do exist and can be developed. We need a small group of individuals with whom we can be ourselves and not be guarded all the time. We need people with whom we can have fun, love and be loved.

Warning! You probably won't find this group of people in a bar! Also, stay clear of groups who find pleasure in gossiping, back-biting, or living shallow lives. You might find a healthy group of people to spend time with in:

a. A recovery group like this
b. In a common-interest club or association
c. A group of peers from work
d. A church

For some, the painful reality may be that you couldn't think of any names to write down in Step 1. Or perhaps you wrote down a few names, but there is no one on the list with whom you could be a confidant. If this is the case for you, it will only serve to intensify your pain and increase your fear. This is no way to live your life, so we will speak about this in more detail next week. There are always other options. There's always hope.

SESSION SEVEN

DAVE'S STORY

Please read the following true story and reflect on the questions that follow.

When I was 22, I reconnected with Dianne, a childhood classmate, whom I had first met in first grade. We had gone through most of primary school together. We began dating the spring of 1980 as she was on the mend from a broken engagement. We soon became inseparable and seemed to have lots in common. I was anxious to move our relationship forward, especially when it came to a physical relationship. I was convinced that we loved each other and rationalized that we would eventually marry anyway.

In the fall of the following year, Dianne broke the news to me that she was pregnant. I immediately panicked! I went into self-preservation mode. While Dianne's parents and I got along well enough, I was intimidated by them and I always felt inadequate around them. I was certain they thought that I wasn't good enough for their daughter and an unexpected pregnancy would certainly prove them right.

I had been raised in a church where image was everything. I had always tried to make sure that no one from church ever saw the rebellious, sinful me. I was ashamed of my predicament and was desperate to protect my image. I was very fearful of what others would think of me.

As I was contemplating my situation, I met with a customer of mine who happened to be an infertility doctor. After we completed our business, I pulled him aside and asked him if he did abortions and what his fee was. I made and paid for the appointment for Dianne.

Immediately, I felt guilty for not stepping up to do the right thing and marry Dianne. Instead, I told her that I had talked to a doctor and had already made arrangements for an abortion. I called her to tell her my plan. I simply and coldly told her, "This is what we should do."

I was in no way equipped for marriage and even less equipped to be a father. If she had decided to keep the baby and we ultimately didn't stay together, I was very uncomfortable about the idea of having a child "out there."

I was in denial about the consequences of this choice, but I had made up my mind that keeping the child was not an option and was dead-set on making her see it my way. I only talked about the bad things a baby would bring into our lives at that point. Dianne was devastated when she realized I wouldn't acquiesce.

I knew that I had let her down. My rationale was all messed up. I reasoned, "If she has the abortion and ends up hating me for it, at least there's no baby in the picture if she ended the relationship." In other words, my image would still be intact as far as everyone else was concerned.

I knew she was afraid of her parents' reaction to her pregnancy as well, so I was pretty sure she wouldn't run to them. I used that to my advantage. I put her in a no-win predicament.

On the day of the abortion, I took off work early and drove Dianne to the doctor. Neither of us spoke a word to or from the doctor's office …

just deafening silence. I was afraid she would talk herself out of going through with it. I knew I had let her down in a major way. I felt ashamed that I had knowingly placed her in a dangerous situation to satisfy my selfish motives.

Both of us lost all of our self-worth that day. What I believed would protect my outward image began to kill my masculinity on the inside. From that day I began to attempt to prove my value as a man, boyfriend and eventually, husband. I was an empty shell of a man.

I pretended that the abortion never happened. But the more I ignored it or tried to make myself forget it, the more the abortion became an ever-present toxin in our relationship.

My coping strategies were completely irrational and futile. I felt compelled to make myself worthy of Dianne's love. I went out of my way to be someone I wasn't and to buy her love with gifts I couldn't afford. I really did love her. But at the same time, I avoided her, because when I was with her my shame reminded me of what I had done to her.

I threw myself into my work, spending long hours there. Then, on the way home I would often stop at a bar to hang out with the guys. I was drinking a lot back then.

I lived in constant shame for getting Dianne pregnant and then forcing her to abort our baby. With the abortion and hurt I had caused Dianne on my conscience, I thought, "Why even try being a good guy?" Indulging in even more destructive behaviors was a way to both punish myself, and try to mask the shame. I felt numb and worthless.

Before we got married, I partied a lot and tried to forget the abortion by filling my life with distractions. But no matter how far away I tried to push the abortion, a simple glance at a billboard, seeing a child, or some commercial on TV would dredge it all right back up again. If I saw Dianne without a smile, I feared she was thinking about the abortion.

In spite of my religious upbringing, I felt unworthy of a relationship with God, with Dianne, or with anyone else. I became more and more distant and closed off from everyone around me. I went to great lengths to try to cover my pain and shame. I couldn't interact normally with people and only engaged in shallow ways. I couldn't let anyone know the real me.

I proposed to Dianne and she said yes. As odd as it sounds, neither Dianne nor I can remember when or how I proposed. We got married in May of 1982. Our first child came along soon after.

During this period, I lived at work. I was very selfish with my time. Soon after our first son was born, I got a new job that took me out of town three-to-four days a week. I remember feeling guilty because I was relieved not to be home much. I didn't have to be reminded about the abortion every day when I looked at my wife and young son.

It wasn't that Dianne brought up the abortion. In fact we never talked about it. Just seeing them was a daily reminder of what I had done. I loved her, but was utterly ashamed of what I'd done to her. Therefore, I got good at avoiding being close-especially when it came to real, intimate conversation. I avoided the things that a strong marriage needs in order to survive.

In 1985, we moved to another city and hoped for a fresh start. Again, I threw myself into my work, routinely spending 60-70 hours a week, in order to avoid going home. Then, after work, I'd stop for a couple of drinks with the guys for an hour or more. I usually drank vodka, so Dianne wouldn't smell it on my breath.

Dianne was very frustrated with our marriage and we always argued. I remember the night that I was forced to see just how selfish and low I had sunk. I was at a bar with the guys drinking. All of a sudden one of the guys elbowed me and gestured toward the door. There was Dianne, making her way to the table as my young son watched from the doorway. I was forced to confront my selfishness. It was now time for me to choose where my life would go from there.

That was really a wakeup call for me. I realized how truly selfish I had been. As a result of that night, I began to try to be more of a husband. I made more of an effort to take the family to church each week. I also cut out my regular stops at the bar after work.

But I remember Dianne telling me, "We're not going to make it. I had an abortion and if we don't talk about it, our marriage won't make it." In an attempt to save our marriage, Dianne scheduled an appointment with someone from church and we went to counseling a couple times. The counselor was direct and while she talked of forgiveness in a generic sort of way, she never dealt with our anger, resentment, or mistrust resulting from the abortion.

Counseling ripped the scab off and made us deal with our wound. We argued a lot about issues caused by the abortion. Dianne hated what I done to her! It was the first time I had heard her verbalize just how deeply I had hurt her. We still hadn't experienced forgiveness, but slowly the ability to dialog opened up between us. Our relationship had a path to begin to change.

Because of my shame, I had always neglected to take a leadership role in the home. How could I be a spiritual leader after the things I had done? I had made a terrible choice by insisting on the abortion and not protecting Dianne and my baby. It left me feeling emasculated. I was not qualified to be the husband.

As we continued to struggle in our marriage, my perception of Dianne's view of me was, "What kind of guy would force me to kill our baby? Why am I even married to him?!" I never felt that I was good enough for her. The topic of divorce was regularly on the table during our struggles and fights. The abortion made great ammunition.

From Dianne's perspective, poor decisions I made or character flaws I had were all magnified through the lens of the abortion. I believed I would never be good enough to be her husband. Our marriage seemed to be based on performance, and because of the abortion, I never quite measured up.

Eventually, Dianne attended a port-abortive class to address the issues from the abortion. Then she went through a second post-abortive Bible study. She was finally able to experience God's forgiveness and healing. She also began to extend forgiveness to me through her actions. I too had asked both Dianne and God to forgive me, but I also felt the need help to process the abortion with other like-minded men.

The Bible study Dianne had experienced also had a curriculum for post-abortive men. I decided to attend. Five of us met in an airplane hangar to work through our abortion experience.

I was amazed to hear that the other guys in my group had all experienced the same things I had after their abortions: excessive drinking, being a workaholic, toxic fights at home, and the need to perform to prove their worth. Again, I saw how deeply I had hurt and scarred Dianne. I had strayed so far from God's ideal as a man, a husband, and a father.

But the post-abortive program put me back on a track to seek God's forgiveness through Christ's death for me on the cross. I began experiencing forgiveness and began gaining back a sense of worth through Christ. For the first time, both Dianne and I felt that with Christ at the center of our lives, we could find healing from the abortion and healing in our marriage.

God has continually bound us together in our marriage and helped us extend grace and love toward each other at times when we felt none. Through Christ, we have experienced forgiveness of sin, but we still struggle at times with the consequences of our sin.

By God's grace, we've been married now for almost 33 years. We've raised three boys and now enjoy three adorable grandchildren. Dianne and I love each other and recently have found tremendous help by praying together daily. Spending time together with God draws us nearer to each other and gives us His perspective to daily live in His love and forgiveness.

—Dave, 2015

DISCUSS DAVE'S STORY

1. In what ways can you identify with Dave's story? What were you feeling?

2. What did Dave do to process his role in an abortion?

3. What can you take away from Dave's story that may help you heal?

SHAME

Shame is a painful emotion caused by a sense of guilt. Shame is a natural and appropriate response to something we've done wrong. The purpose of shame is not to torment us, but to cause us to change. People have a variety of responses to shame. Some may try to "stuff" or "cover" it, while others "beat themselves up" with it, because they feel they deserve it.

Shame is a very common emotion felt by men who've played a role in an abortion. Shame, like some of the other emotions we've covered, causes us to hide, deny, blame others, or rationalize our role in aborting our child. Shame too is debilitating and will prevent us from healing.

Above all, shame breeds a sense of unworthiness. Many post-abortive men express that after their abortion they feel unworthy of the things listed below. Please check all that apply or have applied to you. Many post-abortive men feel unworthy of:

☐ Having children

☐ Being loved by a good woman

☐ Experiencing love and acceptance from others

☐ Receiving or experiencing anything good in life

☐ Other:_____

_____

_____

_____

One way to look at shame and recognize what it does to us is by the following diagram.[29]

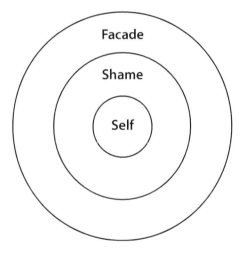

At the center of these concentric circles is our "self" – who we really are. But our shame causes us to hide. By hiding our true self, we cannot be known by others. But in order to establish and maintain relationships, others need to get to know us. So we put up a façade—a false self—to present to others in hopes of being loved and accepted.

---

29   Donald Miller, *Scary Close—Dropping the Act and Finding True Intimacy* (Nashville, TN: Nelson Books, 2014), pp. 20ff.

The problem is that we all know when someone is putting up a false front. We recognize that what they're showing us is not genuine. Others see this in us too. The result is shallow relationships built on pretense. Our shame literally prevents us from loving others fully or being loved by them. Our shame derails our ability to establish meaningful relationships.

The key is to deal with our shame, so we can drop the façade and let others in. In this way, we too can begin to love again and be loved. Only by getting rid of the shame can we hope to build good relationships. So how do we deal with our shame?

At AbAnon, we have found that many men deal with their shame and find healing from their role in an abortion through a relationship with God. AbAnon may not be an overtly religious organization, but we recognize that there is a God and that God is ready and willing to forgive. For this reason we would be remiss if we did not share with you this important remedy for finding freedom from guilt and shame.

If we were to think of shame in terms of physical pain, shame is there to tell us that something is wrong. When we feel shame, it's there to reveal to us that we have done something wrong and we have hurt someone. Shame is very relational.

But shame is also very damning. It does no good to carry shame around with us our entire life. Unfortunately, there's no way we can undo what we have done.

With this in mind, we really only have two choices when it comes to shame. We can either bear its weight and destruction for the rest of our lives; or we can seek forgiveness. When we seek forgiveness, we own up to the wrong we've done. This exposes what we've tried so hard to hide and removes its power over us. When we receive forgiveness, shame is deflated and is replaced with love and acceptance.

In this spirit of forgiveness, we've taken a true story of a man from the Bible named David. Because of some poor decisions, David suffered tremendous failures. But his story demonstrates the power of forgiveness to overcome shame. And David went on to be among the most influential men in history.

THE STORY OF DAVID

David was one of the great, ancient kings of Israel. But he did not come from a royal family. He was the youngest of eight boys. As the youngest, his job was to care for the family's herd of sheep. But David was no ordinary youth. On two different occasions, he had killed a bear and a lion when they came after his sheep. Each time, he chased after the lion and bear and took the sheep from its mouth. And when each beast turned on him, he killed them with a club!

Later, as a man, David's experience with the lion and bear had prepared him for even bigger victories when the enemies of Israel attacked them. David became King over Israel. He was not only a fierce warrior, but led his people with integrity and wisdom.

However, at the peak of his reign, instead of going out to battle with his army, he decided to stay home. One evening he went up to the roof of his palace and looking down from his vantage point, he saw a beautiful woman bathing. As king, he misused his power and sent for her.

David slept with the woman and then sent her back home. But a short while later, she sent a message to David telling him she was pregnant. Now David had a serious problem, because it turned out that the woman's husband was one of David's chief fighting men. And for some time, her husband had been away from home at war. There was no way her child could be her husband's.

Again, because he had the authority to do so, David sent a messenger to the battle lines and called the woman's husband home. David hoped that he would come home, sleep with his wife and assume the baby was his.

But when her husband reported to David, he was so focused on his mission that he refused to enjoy the comfort of his home and his wife's embrace while his comrades were dying in battle. When David saw that his plan had failed, he wrote a letter to his general instructing him to put this man on the front lines in a way that would guarantee his death. David sent this sealed message with the woman's husband!

In this way, David murdered the woman's husband and then took her to become his wife. In the months that followed, before the woman gave birth, David managed to hide his adultery and murder. He went on with his life and no one was the wiser...or so he thought.

But God knew what David had done and sent Nathan, David's friend and counselor, to confront him. The reality of what he had done hit David with the full force of the guilt and shame that resulted from sleeping with another man's wife and then murdering him to cover up his deed. There was no way to undo what he had done.

Of course, as king, David could have used his influence to continue his cover-up. But David chose a different path to deal with the guilt and shame he now felt over what he'd done. David knew that he needed to be forgiven. He couldn't seek forgiveness from the man he had killed. Perhaps he asked his new wife to forgive him, though it's likely she was as much to blame as he was.

The only one David could turn to for forgiveness was God. Now confronted with the crushing weight of his shame and guilt, David acknowledged his sin against God and begged God's forgiveness. And God forgave him, removing his guilt and shame.

God knows you just as thoroughly as He knew David. He knows everything you have ever done. He knows about your involvement in abortion. The guilt and shame you feel negate any justification you might raise for the abortion. But God makes that same offer of forgiveness to you that He made to David. He knows your shame and offers to remove it from you.

TAKE ACTION

Shame causes us to hide, deny, blame others and justify our role in the abortion. In shame we provide others with a façade, because we are ashamed to reveal our true self. Unless dealt with, shame will prevent us from ever healing or experiencing meaningful relationships. Ironically, shame prevents us from exposing our role in the abortion, but it's only by exposing our abortion role that we gain freedom from shame.

Hiding our shame intensifies it and prolongs our agony. When we reveal and renounce our shame, we find forgiveness and healing. Out of a love for us we'll never truly understand, God sent His Son Jesus to die for our sins. He bore our guilt and shame on Himself when He was crucified. Jesus was buried and on the third day rose from the dead, proving that His life was more than sufficient to pay for our sins. He offers us forgiveness from our sins, thereby delivering us from the crushing weight of guilt and shame.

Like David from long ago, many post-abortive men have found freedom from guilt and shame by trusting Jesus Christ and receiving His forgiveness. If you would like to trust Jesus Christ and receive His forgiveness, simply pray to Him. Confess your sins to Him and ask Him to forgive you. He doesn't turn anyone away. He loves you and offers you healing.

If as a result of reading this you have put your trust in Christ, please tell your facilitator that you have made this decision. Regardless of whether you choose to put your trust in Christ, we are here to love you and walk with you through your healing process.

SESSION EIGHT

KEVIN'S STORY

Please read the following true story and reflect on the questions that follow.

Five months ago, I received a message on Facebook from a former girl-friend, "Hi, Kevin this is Debbie. I was just thinking about you and wanted to catch up. Quite often I think about our child. If he had been born, he'd be 21 years old today."

Debbie's message hit me like a ton of bricks! Our abortion was an incident that I had stuffed for over two decades. I had totally packed it away. But hearing from Debbie and sensing the regret in her voice totally took me by surprise. Out of nowhere, our abortion became heavy on my heart.

I had grown up in a religious family and as a kid attended church with a close family friend. When I was around 11 years old, I went to church camp and accepted Christ into my heart. But during my high school and college years I completely stopped going to church.

In college I pursued a science degree majoring in physiology and anatomy. I proceeded to live a very promiscuous life, jumping from girlfriend to girlfriend. One such girl was Debbie. I met her at a bar where she bartended.

Debbie and I had been going together for about six months when she announced that she was pregnant. She already had a three-year-old son from a previous marriage and shared 50/50 custody with her x-husband. Together, Debbie and I decided that neither of us was ready in our relationship to take on another child. I was very selfish not wanting to commit to her or the baby.

The abortion was a mutual decision. She set up the appointment and I drove her to the clinic, but did not go in with her for the procedure. After the procedure, she was sad for some time. We dated perhaps another six or seven months before she moved out-of-state and we broke up.

Years passed and I met my wife, Carol, and we married three years later. She seemed to be surrounded by Christian women in the hospital ICU unit where she worked as a nurse. She didn't come from a Christian background, but her Christian co-workers convinced her to at least listen to the message of Christ so our kids would be exposed.

One evening Carol asked me about my beliefs. Her question hit me at a time when I had been considering returning to the church for no other reason than I felt called back. A short time later, we joined an evangelical church where many of the cops I worked with attended. There, Carol and I committed our lives to Christ again. But it wasn't until about five years later (around 2008) that we were baptized. Christ has made a huge positive difference in our marriage and family as we raise our children.

But when Debbie reconnected with me five months ago, it turned my world upside down. Via Facebook, I confessed to her that if I could do it over again, I would not choose to abort our child. She wrote back, "Neither would I."

Since Debbie's message regarding our abortion, I've experienced a lot of sadness and regret. For some reason, Debbie and I both think of our baby as a boy. I constantly wonder what he would look like—what he would be like. While the abortion seemed like the right thing to do at the time, it has only made both of us very sad and full of regret. I'm greatly disappointed in myself today for choosing the path that we did.

Reflecting back on this incident made me realize that I'm probably responsible for at least one other abortion with another woman. This has only intensified my feelings of sadness and regret.

Since the abortion, I have served as a firefighter, emergency medical responder, and police officer. During those years, I witnessed a lot of really bad stuff. I saw things that most people can't even imagine. The automobile accidents, knifings, shootings, and especially the child abuse and neglect were awful! I've seen so much death and have come to cherish how precious life is.

On numerous occasions, I've performed CPR on a child who was in the throes of death. Those faces and memories are indelibly engraved on my mind. As a result, I've become an ardent protector of children. I can't stand to see a helpless child suffer at the hands of an adult's stupidity and poor choices. I don't think you can really value life until you've seen it so devalued.

For some years now, I've worked in the medical profession. I've made it my goal to save and preserve life. This makes my involvement in my past abortions even more abhorrent to me. Without Christ's mercy and forgiveness, I honestly don't know how I'd cope with the guilt!

—Kevin, 2016

DISCUSS DANIEL'S STORY

1. In what ways can you identify with Kevin's story? What were you feeling?

2. What did Kevin do to process his role in an abortion?

3. What can you take away from Kevin's story that may help you heal?

BRINGING CLOSURE TO YOUR GRIEF

Although you may not have thought about the abortion this way in the past, you now recognize that you have lost a loved one. Parents who experience a miscarriage, especially later in their pregnancy, also experience grief over the loss of their child.

Grief is a natural and healthy response to great loss. Grief expresses itself in sadness, a sense of deep loss, and mourning. Grief may numb us or overwhelm us. We may feel "lost" or experience a profound sense of emptiness.

Normally, when a loved one passes away, we find consolation and closure through a formal memorial service or funeral. Even though it's difficult to attend such an event, the experience helps us come to grips with reality and initiates healing over our grief that otherwise might not occur.

One thing that makes a miscarried baby or an abortion so difficult to heal from is that we are usually denied the opportunity to formally grieve or provide some kind of memorial for that little one. There has been no closure. We grieve internally, but we have no healthy release for our grief.

As we've already noted, our culture suppresses the humanity and personhood of an aborted child. In doing so, this denies us the freedom to grieve and certainly denounces the need to observe some kind of memorial service for our child.

When we speak of "closure" over our grief, this does not mean that we will never grieve again over our lost child. But it does mean that we've initiated a clear course of action to ascribe dignity and worth to our child, thereby giving credence and voice to our grief.

Many post-abortive men and women have found great release from their grief and sorrow by making a conscious effort to remember their child in a dignified manner—in a way worthy of a human being. There is no recommended protocol for doing this, but it should be something that you feel will be meaningful to you and honoring to your baby.

For example, many post-abortive men and women have found closure to their grief by naming their child. Naming the baby attaches personhood to him or her. Others might plant a tree as a remembrance, give a memorial gift to a charity, buy a solitary rose and dry or press it to preserve it, or purchase a special necklace or ring to wear in remembrance of their child. The important thing is to find something that holds meaning for you.

THE ETERNAL NATURE OF THE HUMAN SOUL

God reveals in the Bible that death is not final for a human being. We believe that we will see our aborted babies again. And because of Christ's forgiveness, that reunion with our child will be sweet and joyful, not bitter or sorrowful.

The Power of Your Story for Men

In view of this, one other action that has proven very therapeutic and cathartic for post-abortive men and women is to write a short note or letter to their baby. In it they may express their love and sorrow; ask forgiveness; talk about meeting them one day; and anything else they deem meaningful to write.

Of course, this note or letter won't go anywhere, but it would be one more way of honoring your child and ascribing to him or her their humanity and worth.

TAKING STOCK

Here again are the "Taking Stock" statements that we saw in Session Three. You have been through much over the past few weeks and it would be valuable for you to see where you are in relationship to where you've been. As before, this "Taking Stock" process includes fifteen statements, each followed by these word choices: Strongly Agree, Agree, Not Sure, Disagree and Strongly Disagree. Feel free to use the same responses that you used in Session Three or respond differently if you feel anything has changed.

1. I have made more than my share of impulsive decisions that I later regretted making.

    Strongly Agree   Agree   Not Sure   Disagree   Strongly Disagree

2. I have usually had the self-control I needed to keep me from doing things I later regret.

    Strongly Agree   Agree   Not Sure   Disagree   Strongly Disagree

3. I stay angry longer than I think is healthy for me.

    Strongly Agree   Agree   Not Sure   Disagree   Strongly Disagree

4. I have forgiven the people who have done the most
    harm to me.

    Strongly Agree   Agree   Not Sure   Disagree   Strongly Disagree

5. I struggle with addictive substances.

    Strongly Agree   Agree   Not Sure   Disagree   Strongly Disagree

6. I struggle with addictive behaviors.

    Strongly Agree   Agree   Not Sure   Disagree   Strongly Disagree

7. I have achieved the goals I expected to reach by this
    point in my life.

    Strongly Agree   Agree   Not Sure   Disagree   Strongly Disagree

8. I feel hopeful about the future.

    Strongly Agree   Agree   Not Sure   Disagree   Strongly Disagree

9. I have at least one trusted and reliable friend I can turn
    to in time of need.

    Strongly Agree   Agree   Not Sure   Disagree   Strongly Disagree

10. I take responsibility for being where I am today, and I do
    not blame anyone else.

    Strongly Agree   Agree   Not Sure   Disagree   Strongly Disagree

11. I have suffered serious trauma in my life and feel I have
    not really gotten over it.

    Strongly Agree   Agree   Not Sure   Disagree   Strongly Disagree

12. I wish I had a deeper spiritual life or connection with God.

    Strongly Agree   Agree   Not Sure   Disagree   Strongly Disagree

13. I feel like I keep making the same mistakes and bad
    decisions again and again.

    Strongly Agree   Agree   Not Sure   Disagree   Strongly Disagree

14. I have a strong sense of right and wrong that I think most people would agree with.

    Strongly Agree   Agree   Not Sure   Disagree   Strongly Disagree

15. I have had an experience in my life that still causes me to feel shame when I think about it.

    Strongly Agree   Agree   Not Sure   Disagree   Strongly Disagree

TAKE ACTION

We ask that you complete three specific tasks this week. Because of the nature of two of these tasks, you won't want to leave them for the last moment before attending Session Eight.

Please write a short note or letter to your aborted child or children. This letter or note is for your eyes only, unless you choose to share it with others.

In addition to the note or letter, think of some meaningful way to establish a memorial for your child. This is a very personal exercise. It does not matter what someone else does. You choose something that is most meaningful to you in remembering your child and bringing closure to their death. Some men may wish to perform this exercise with their confidant or another trusted individual.

One of the reasons that our culture fails to recognize the reality of post abortion stress syndrome is the lack of testimony by men and women who have experienced it. Abortion Anonymous (AbAnon) and the community of tens of millions of post-abortive men and women would be very grateful if you would take a few minutes to **complete an anonymous survey** that we are conducting. This survey will help us demonstrate to the world the harm that abortion causes women and men. **The survey will only take you a few minutes and is completely anonymous. Your Group Facilitator will provide you**

SESSION EIGHT

a copy of the survey or you can go to the following web address to take the *survey online: www.AbAnon.org/survey.* Thank you.

ADDITIONAL STEPS FOR HEALING

Our hope and prayer is that this curriculum has at the very least helped contribute to your healing process. Healing from an abortion is no small matter and often requires more than one or two experiences like this. Please let us know how we can serve you to help further your healing process. Following are some suggested next steps:

1. Continue to meet with your **confidant** on a weekly basis.

2. Meet with a **mentor** for a period of time. A mentor is usually a man who has been through the AbAnon curriculum and has experienced a measure of healing. He has volunteered to work with other post-abortive men to help them in their healing process.

3. Join another post-abortive **small group** session like this one.

    a. You are welcome to go through this experience again with another group.
    b. Or, we can assist you to find another group with a different curriculum to further promote your healing.

4. If you would like to deepen your relationship with Jesus Christ, please let us know and we can help facilitate this as well.

5. If you would like to hear more about God and Jesus Christ, please let us know and we can provide additional resources and opportunities for you.

Made in the USA
San Bernardino, CA
03 February 2017